Anonymous

Atlantic City and County, New Jersey

Anonymous

Atlantic City and County, New Jersey

ISBN/EAN: 9783337216610

Printed in Europe, USA, Canada, Australia, Japan

Cover: Foto ©ninafisch / pixelio.de

More available books at **www.hansebooks.com**

Atlantic City
and County

∴ ∴ New Jersey ∴ ∴
∴ Biographically Illustrated ∴

A short biography, illustrated
by portraits, of prominent residents of Atlantic County and
the famous summer and winter
resort, celebrated throughout
America– Atlantic City. ∴ ∴

Alfred M. Slocum Co. ∴ Printers
and Publishers ∴ 718-724 Arch St.
∴ ∴ Philadelphia ∴ ∴ [1899 ∴

IN OFFERING this volume to the public the publishers feel they present an unusually attractive field to the many admirers of the famous seaside resort, Atlantic City. The object throughout has been to introduce, by means of short biographies, accompanied with portraits, a number of prominent residents of Atlantic City and County, making a permanent Souvenir, which we feel will add value to the pleasant past associations which this delightful locality has given so many. As a matter of history and local interest this book has unusual value, preserving in complete form memories of many prominent people who have stamped their individuality upon the past events of their town.

The publishers have aimed to secure accurate information and to arrange their data in such attractive form as may increase its usefulness in every sense.

ALFRED M. SLOCUM CO.
PUBLISHERS

Philadelphia, Pa.
1899

Introductory.

"ATLANTIC CITY AND COUNTY," biographically illustrated, is a combination of history and biography. The life of the locality and the story of the individual are inseparably connected, for local history and biography are the perfect analysis of kindred topics, and in a general sense most valuable as an intelligent study of events, conditions and people which constitute a most comprehensive view of the national existence of yesterday and to-day.

This history particularly pertains to a wonderful and original city and embodies the outside influences which have contributed largely to its success, and attempts a summary of the many details of unknown or forgotten events, which in the broad light of the present assume their proper importance as factors in the fulfilment of the Atlantic City of 1899, and lead with unerring judgment the progressive movement for future success and greatness.

The history of the past is the record of the few, unfortunately forgotten by the residents of the present generation, who, in their earnest struggle of to-day, are progressively pushing forward against tremendous competition for that substantial benefit which, in the opinion of philosophers, if successful, creates a like advantage to the community as well as the individual;

Introductory

wherefore the history of the present is the record of the many, to whom the future holds out its infinite promise of success, and in no locality does that future seem fraught with happier conditions than Atlantic City and surroundings.

This seaside city is, without doubt, the most famous resort in the fair state of New Jersey, and has established itself upon a permanent basis entirely different from other like resorts; in fact the historian must approach conditions here without the advantage or use of former time-honored methods, for this is a city created by unusual opportunities, readily seized upon and wrought out by "brainy men, who have builded better than they knew," and to-day, from all over the country, deep in the hearts of its countless sojourners, there exists a warm and tender regard for the City by the Sea. Romance and reality have both been important factors in this respect, as the child, maiden, lover, invalid, physician, and many a business man will testify in their unstinted praise for the special relief they represent.

A careful study has been given to the medical, political, judicial, financial, educational, religious and social matters, principally compiled from articles furnished by eminent local authorities.

Produced by a vast amount of careful and diligent labor this work supplies a general and permanent need, and its information will not become obsolete through future change and progress, as it preserves the value of the past and present for the advantage of the future.

The compilation of this work has been entrusted to Mr. Frank H. Taylor, whose reputation as artist and author requires no introduction from us—and the publishers are confident that the following pages will constitute not only an attractive souvenir of descriptive art, but also an invaluable record of lasting usefulness. We beg, also, to express our appreciation of the valuable assistance of Mr. A. M. Heston, City Controller of Atlantic City and publisher of Heston's Hand Book; for the aid rendered by Mr. A. H. Mueller, of Philadelphia, publisher of the very accurate atlas of Atlantic City recently completed; and our thanks are also due to the many officials and citizens who have bestowed upon our undertaking their aid and patronage.

ALFRED M. SLOCUM CO.
PUBLISHERS

Philadelphia, Pa.
1899

Contents

CHAPTER I.
HISTORICAL SKETCH . . . . Page 17
In Olden Days—The Harbor of Eggs—A Highway of the Revolution—The Story of Commander Somers—Our Early Navy—A Naval Exploit of Note—A Sad but Heroic Ending—The Gallant Hobson—St. George's, Bermuda—People of the Coast—A Legend—The Drinks of our Forefathers—A Shore County—First Hotels.

CHAPTER II.
THE OLD SHORE ROAD . . . . Page 29
An Early Type—Natives Inland—Quiet Highways—Jersey Arcadia—Along the Road.

CHAPTER III.
THE BIRTH OF A CITY . . . . Page 33
The Camden & Atlantic Railroad—A Gloomy Prospect—When Speech was Golden—The Opening Wedge—The First Through Train—Through by Rail—Success Assured—The Survey and Naming of Atlantic City—An Early Impression—In 1879—Nature's Great Physician.

CHAPTER IV.
FIRST ADMINISTRATION . . . . Page 45
Early Hotels of Atlantic City—Railroad Progress—The Present Era—A Noted Comfort—Atlantic City Twenty-five Years Ago—Happy Days—The Higbee Club—The Border of the Deep.

CHAPTER V.
THE RESTLESS SEA . . . . Page 54
Rivers of the Sea—Facts from Heston's Hand-Book.

CHAPTER VI.
THE BOARDWALK . . . . Page 59
  The Pleasure Piers—Boardwalk Glimpses—The Summer Multitudes.

CHAPTER VII.
ATLANTIC AVENUE . . . . Page 67
  A Great Business Thoroughfare—Pacific Avenue—In the Suburbs—A Pleasant Round Trip—Room to Spread—A Friendly Call—About Advertising—Bygone Discomforts—A Forecast—Cycling to the Sea—A Port of Entry—An Aquarium—A Port of the Manx—An English Resort—Make People Talk.

CHAPTER VIII.
THE PLEASURE FLEET AT THE INLET . . . . Page 82
  Upon a Summer Morn—Old Favorites—The Fleet of '98.

CHAPTER IX.
A REFUGE FROM ILLNESS AND CARE . . . . Page 86
  A Health Record—Winter Hospitality.

CHAPTER X.
IN PRIVATE COTTAGES . . . . Page 88
  Ideal Existence—Palatial Homes.

CHAPTER XI.
THE COUNTRY CLUB . . . . Page 90
  A Social Centre—Many Comforts—The Stables—The Pines—Varied Sports.

CHAPTER XII.
THE LENTEN SEASON . . . . Page 94
  The Awakening—The Joyous Sea—Cycle Road to Atlantic City.

CHAPTER XIII.
SOME CITY MATTERS . . . . Page 97
  Values and Finances from Report of 1898—The Fire Fighters—Light and Water—Sewerage—Military—At the Nation's Call.

CHAPTER XIV.

CHILDREN'S SEASHORE HOUSE . . . . Page 100
A Splendid Charity—For Young and Old—The Story of an Old Man—Return to Simplicity—In Business by the Sea.

CHAPTER XV.

ALONG THE BOARDWALK . . . . Page 104
A Healthy Spot—The Unprofitable Sign—On Rollers—The Gamins of the Beach—Evening Scenes—Love by the Sea.

CHAPTER XVI.

OFF DAYS AT THE SHORE . . . . Page 111
In the Drifts—The Flow of Enjoyments—Sunny Corners—Rainy Day Philosophy—The Stormy Sea.

CHAPTER XVII.

THE BOROUGH OF LONGPORT . . . . Page 115
A Great Drive—Advantages—Beautiful Homes—A Review—Natural Science—Hotels and Clubs—The Ferry—Borough Officials—Seashore Joys—In Spring—Autumn—Winter—Joys of Longport—The Thoroughfare—The Lower Inlet—In Late Autumn.

CHAPTER XVIII.

LIGHT-HOUSES . . . . Page 135
Antiquity of Beacons—A Noble Beacon—View from the Tower—Little Egg Harbor Inlet—Channel Leading into Great Harbor Inlet and Bay above Somers' Point.

CHAPTER XIX.

THE LIFE-SAVING SERVICE AND WRECKS . . . . . Page 141
The Atlantic City Station—Statistics—Ship Ashore—Famous Wrecks—The Love Letter—The Message in a Bottle—List of Casualties to Vessels—List of Life-Saving Stations—Absecon Inlet and Bay above Anchorage to Brigantine Wharf.

CHAPTER XX.

ABORIGINAL FOOTPRINTS . . . . Page 156
An Indian Home—Reading the Past—What Did They Eat?—A Lotus Land—A List of Game.

CHAPTER XXI.

A PLATE OF ABSECONS . . . . Page 162
The Struggle of Life—Ancient Oyster Beds—Some Calculations.

CHAPTER XXII.

A PEN PICTURE OF THE BEACH . . . . Page 167
The Tides of Life—A Word on the East Wind—A Boisterous Friend—The Floor of the Sea.

CHAPTER XXIII.

THE FASTEST TRAIN . . . . Page 173
A Run to the Shore—The Big Engine—The Start—In the Cab—Over Seventy Miles an Hour.

CHAPTER XXIV.

ATLANTIC CITY AS A WINTER AND SPRING RESORT . . Page 178
The Gulf Stream—The Music of the Surf—A Pen Picture—A Round of Pleasure—For Invalids—Schools, Churches and Charities.

CHAPTER XXV.

PENNA. R. R. ROUTES TO THE COAST . . . . Page 184

CHAPTER XXVI.

ATLANTIC CITY HORSE SHOW ASSOCIATION . . Page 187

CHAPTER XXVII.

THE CLIMATE OF ATLANTIC CITY AND ITS USEFULNESS IN DISEASE . . . . Page 189
Distinguished Testimony—A Mistaken Idea—Comparison of Temperature—Days Bright and Sunny—Professor Bache's Conclusions—Formation of the Gulf Stream—Evaporation and Precipitation—Tonic and Alterative Climate—Immunity from Hay Fever.

Index
Biographical
Sketches

	PAGE
ADAMS, I. G. . . .	cli
ADAMS, LEWIS R. . . .	cxxix
ALBERTSON, DANIEL L. . .	lxxiii
ALBERTSON, LEVI C. . . .	xix
BANEY, H. C. . . .	clxiii
BARTON, SAMUEL	clix
BELL, WILLIAM A.	clxxiii
BRYANT, MAJOR LEWIS T. . .	lxv
CONROW, ROLAND	xcix
CRANDALL, DR. J. F.	lvii
CURRIE, GEORGE F. . . .	xvii
DALEY, JAMES	cxxxv
DARNALL, WILLIAM EDGAR, A. B., M. D. .	li
DEVINE, MICHAEL A. . . .	xxxvii
DICKINSON, THOMAS J. .	cxlvii
DONNELLY, JOHN	cxix
DOWN, LORENZO A. . . .	xxi
EDGE, WALTER E. . .	lxi
EDWARDS, DEVOUX B. . .	xcv
ELDRIDGE, HENRY C.	cxiii
ENDICOTT, HON. ALLEN B. . .	xiii
EVANS, HON. CHARLES .	xv
EVANS, HON. LEWIS	xxiii

Index
Biographical
Sketches

	PAGE
FEDIGAN, REV. J. J., O. S. A.	cxxxvii
FELKER, GEORGE C.	cxliii
GALE, SAMUEL P.	cxxvii
GARRABRANT, C., M. D.	clxvii
GENEROTZKY, WILLIAM G.	cxxxi
GODFREY, BURROWS C.	xxxi
GODFREY, CARLTON, ESQ.	xxix
GORMAN, JOHN L.	clxxiv
GOULDEY, JOHN	lxxi
GROSS, THEO.	clxv
GUTTRIDGE, OLIVER H.	cvii
HARRIS, HOWARD G., C. E.	ciii
HESTON, ALFRED M.	xxvii
INGERSOLL, JUDGE ROBERT H.	xxxix
IRELAN, EMERY D.	cxlix
JOHNSON, C. G.	cxi
JOHNSON, WILLIAM N.	xliii
JONES, WILLIAM P.	lxxix
JORDAN, ALBERT M.	cix
KELLEY, SAMUEL HASTINGS	xxxv
LEE, EDWARD S.	cxxxix
LEEDS, CHALKLEY S.	v
LEEDS, ROBERT L.	lxxv
LONG, GEORGE H.	clxi
McCANN, HERBERT	clxxii
McLAUGHLAN, WILLIAM	lxiii
MEHRER, JOHN E.	lxxxi
MERCHANT, OLIVER	cxxv
MIDDLETON, FRANK	cv
MOORE, I. WILDEN	xcvii
MOORE, SAMUEL W.	cxxi
MORRIS, DANIEL	vii
MUELLER, JACOB	cxxiii

MYERS, CHARLES R.
MYERS, DANIEL W.
MYERS, JACOB C.
MYERS, JOHN
NORTH, JAMES, M. D., D. D. S.
PERKINS, COL. GEORGE H.
REED, THOMAS K.
ROCHFORD, J. J.
ROSE, S. B.
SCHWEISFORT, S. A.
SCOTT, LEWIS PENNINGTON
SEEDS, DR. WM. FRANCIS
SHERRICK, HARRY W.
SHREVE, JOHN G.
SMITH, EDWIN
SMITH, FRANK A.
SMITH, J. C.
SOUDER, FRANK A.
SOUTHWICK, JAMES D.
SPEIDEL, CHARLES M.
STEWART, WM. BLAIR, M. D.
STIMSON, GILBERT S.
STOY, HON. F. P.
TAYLOR, S. C.
THOMPSON, HON. JOSEPH
VOELKER, CARL
WAHL, WILLIAM F.
WALTON, M.
WILLIAMSON, BENJAMIN
WILSON, THOMAS K.
WOOTON, HARRY
WRIGHT, ELIAS
YOUNG, JOHN L.

Atlantic City. Chapter I.

 The story of Atlantic City is a part of the annals of our own generation; it chronicles an achievement, typical **Historical Sketch** in its magnitude and character, of the resistless second half of the greatest of all the centuries.

Summer resorts have existed from the beginning of civilization. Beside the purple bays of the Orient, for thousands of years, tired humanity has been lulled to rest to the music of splashing waters. Babies have disported, while youths and maidens have loved, and men and women have forgotten the vexations of life in the sensuous allurements of the passing hour. But there has never before, in all the ages, existed an Atlantic City.

As an effective background to the picture of our great "City by the Sea," it is proper to sketch, in the briefest way, the outline of the development of a Commonwealth from the crude materials of a region which remained essentially a wilderness for more than a century after the Colonies of the Cavaliers were well advanced along the James River, and the Puritans of Massachusetts Bay had established there the foundations of a Province of enduring influence.

New Jersey has a history peculiar to itself. All of this domain having been, in the first instance, held by right of discovery by the English, was wrested from them by the energetic mariners of the ships from the

Holland States, who dominated the territory from the settlement of *Nieu Amstel*, or New Amsterdam, the Dutch immigrants spreading forth from this citadel, as they came in frequent shiploads, into the present counties of Bergen, Essex, Monmouth, Somerset and Middlesex, a portion of the State which carries the impress of their influence to the present day.

In 1664 the English came in force and expelled the government of the Dutch, and Governor Stuyvesant's "New Netherlands" was blotted from the map of Holland's Colonial possessions. Closely following, was written, by the hand of Charles II, the all important Royal Patent, granting this broad territory to his brother James, then Duke of York, and afterwards the successor of Charles. All titles to lands have, in this transaction, their foundation stone.

In Olden Days

In turn the Duke of York conveyed this far-away wilderness to Lord Berkeley and Sir George Carteret, in payment of the political debt due their loyalty in the course of the Civil War. Carteret, who had been Governor of the Isle of Jersey, proposed the name of New Jersey for their joint domain.

In 1675, John Fenwick and Edward Byllinge, who had settled at Salem, had succeeded to the rights of Lord Berkeley, and upon July 1st of the next year, at a conference in the City of London between Sir George Carteret upon one hand, and William Penn, Gawden Lawrie, Nicholas Lucas and Edward Byllinge upon the other, as Trustees, a line was agreed upon defining the boundary between the Jerseys. Said line running from a point upon the upper Delaware River, below the site of Port Jervis, "to the most southernly point of the east side of Little Egg Harbor Bay." Sixty-seven years later this line was corrected and reaffirmed by John Lawrence, Surveyor, its location being upon the longitude of 41° and 40 min. These sections were denominated respectively East and West New Jersey. The Executors of Sir George Carteret eventually disposed of this property to twelve persons, who, in turn, sold a half interest to twelve others, all of whom were known as its proprietors.

An interesting old map of the Jerseys gives a fair idea of the extent to which European civilization had leavened the lump of New Jersey's wilderness in the year 1769, when it was prepared by Lieutenant Bernard Ratzer, of the 60th Regiment, English. A vast tract to the west of the division line drawn between East and West New Jersey was an untrodden wilderness. Within the present confines of the County of Atlantic, a single pathway, the Old Shore Road extended, having its beginning near Little Egg Harbor, where it joined a cross country road from Burlington, and extending down the coast to Cape May. The only settlement was Leeds. It was here, perhaps, that the early settlers lived who attracted the first official notice of the Provisional Assembly, the record of which appears in the proceedings of the session of 1694, in the following words: "Forasmuch as there are some families settled upon Egg Harbor, and of right ought to be under some jurisdiction, be it enacted, that by the authority aforesaid, the inhabitants of said Egg Harbor, shall and do belong to the jurisdiction of Gloucester, to all intents and purposes, till such time as they shall be capable by competent number of inhabitants to be erected into a county, any former act to the contrary notwithstanding."

Egg Harbor had gained its name from the vast numbers of eggs of wild fowl noted there by the Dutch explorers, who called it "Eyer Haven." By the early English settlers it was also known as New Weymouth, but time has perpetuated its quaint, and doubtless earlier cognomen. This ancient "Egg Harbor," set upon the winding channel back from its bay some miles to the north of the modern station of the name, may be counted, therefore, as the first seat of white settlement within the present county. A few years after the issue of the foregoing edict, tithing officers were sent to the Egg Harbor settlement by the Gloucester County authorities, although the legal right to do so has been since brought into question, as the coast district was not regularly engrafted upon that county until 1710, and for a long period all of what is now Atlantic County was

The Harbor
of Eggs

19

known generally as the " Egg Harbor region." The townships of Galloway, Gloucestertown and Woolwich were created therefrom, the name of Galloway first appearing upon the county records in March, 1775. This name is believed to have been derived from that of a tongue of land at Solloway Firth, Scotland, called Galloway Mull.

One Gabriel Thomas, an early traveler through this strip of coast, wrote that ships of two or three hundred tons might navigate the great Egg Harbor River, and that the country round about was famous for plenty of corn, as well as horses, cows, sheep, hogs and other evidences of prosperity, but preacher John Fothergill, who labored in this wildwood vineyard in 1722, called his experience a "journey through a desart," having had a particularly rough time by field and flood.

THE MARSHES.

Over upon great Egg Harbor, a group of settlers was huddled around Somers' Point, and a considerable business was doubtless done in the cutting and shipping upon small vessels of timber and firewood, for George May built a store at the landing still bearing his name, in the year 1710, for the accommodation of the skippers and crew. May's house was still standing as late as 1830, upon the bank of the winding little stream, a few rods above Babcock's Creek.

During the period of the Revolution, Egg Harbor seems to have fully maintained its reputation as a lively spot. Richard Westcott and Elijah Clark built a fort upon Chestnut Neck, dominating the stream, and manned it with cannon at their own expense. It was called "the Foxburrows Fort." The New Jersey authorities bought it from them in 1777, for £430 1s. 3d. sterling. A British force landed here in 1778 and effected considerable destruction. Privateers sailed in and out of these harbors, and there was much coming and going of both royalists and whigs. British

A Highway of the Revolution

prisoners escaped from the cantonment in Virginia, later in the war, were harbored here and helped on their way to New York. There was much thrifty traffic with the British masters of Philadelphia in supplies carried in stealthy expeditions through the woods to the Delaware River. The majority of the people were, however, sound rebels, and the rolls of the Revolutionary forces contain many names of the men of Absecon who played the patriot's part. For some time a company of Continentals was stationed here to close this gateway of traffic and travel to the enemy, and some skirmishing occurred.

In the war with Great Britain, beginning in 1812, the Somers' Point people distinguished themselves. In 1813 the sloop *New Jersey* from that port was captured by an armed British schooner off Cape May, and a prize crew put on board. Captain Barton and his two men overcame the captors and brought them into Somers' Point, doubtless with great *éclat*.

The summer loiterer at old Somers' Point may wander from the huddle of hotels and club-houses at the wharf back among the pines, along a winding and sandy by-way, until he comes into view of the old Somers' homestead.

This was the birthplace of a hero. It is generally said to be the oldest house in Atlantic County. It is a quaint and rambling trio of structures, still occupied upon rental. The "new part" was built about a century since, and the oldest section, with its huge chimney, was doubtless reared by John Somers soon after his purchase of this plantation of 3000 acres from Thomas Budd in 1795, and it was here that Richard, his son, brought his beautiful young bride, Judith, the daughter of Sir James Letart, of Acadia, whose adopted father, Peter White, had moved to Absecon.

The Story of Commander Somers

The Somers family always held an active part in the affairs of the central New Jersey coast, and the French strain in their blood impelled them constantly to that abundant field of adventure, the convenient sea.

THE OLD
SOMERS
HOMESTEAD

whose breakers were ever within sight of their windows. Colonel Richard Somers, the second, was active upon the side of the patriots in the period of the Revolution, and it was during this fateful era, September 15, 1778, that the third Richard Somers, the lost hero of Tripoli, was born. Like all of the amphibious youth of the coast, this member of the fourth Somers generation took to the water almost in his babyhood, and, as a handy boy, he sailed upon coasters to and from the ports of New York and Philadelphia. Then he took to the navy, and at the age of twenty had won his warrant as midshipman upon the grand old frigate United States, of forty-four guns, the flagship of Commodore John Barry.

Our Early Navy   In that year, the Ganges, twenty-four guns; the Constellation, twenty-eight guns, and the Delaware, twenty guns, had hastened away ahead of the flagship in hot chase of the French privateers, which ravaged our coasts. The United States, built and equipped in Philadelphia, sailed in July. A messmate of Somers was the midshipman, Stephen Decatur. In the following year, after many adventures, Somers was made third Lieutenant, and in 1800, second Lieutenant. The "Old Wagoner," as the United States was called, cruised far and wide. Many of our early naval heroes were graduates of her decks. In the year 1801 this famous ship was laid up until a dozen years later she was called into service by the exigencies of the War of 1812-14. Upon her retirement, young Somers became first Lieutenant of the frigate Boston, a twenty-eighter, celebrated at the time as the captor of the heavy French corvette Bercean. The Boston was sent to the Mediterranean with orders to join the squadron operating there. In the following year the Boston came home, and, under the reduction law then applied to the navy, through the workings of the economies of the time, she was laid up to rot in her berth. But one vessel below the rate of frigate, the Enterprise, of twelve guns, was kept in service, but of four new ships of war ordered by Congress, Somers was given command of the Nautilus. She was a beautiful schooner, mounting twelve carronades and a couple of sixes, with a crew of from eighty to ninety all told.

It was Preble's squadron that sailed away to chastise the pirates of the Algerine coast, and the Nautilus led the expedition, followed at brief intervals by the Constitution, the flagship ; the Philadelphia, the Argus, the Siren, the Vixen, and the Enterprise. All met at Gibraltar, then over they sailed to Morocco, and the Philadelphia, with the Vixen, was sent on to blockade Tripoli.

Presently the whole fleet were sailing up and down in front of the capital of the troublesome Bashaw, all but the Philadelphia, which had been bagged by the old pirate, and her crew sent into bondage. The reefs of the difficult harbor gleamed through the breakers like the teeth of a tiger in a cave, and many were the projects born in the cabins of the American ships to get at the batteries and gunboats of the corsairs. In the course of a hot fight one August day, the frigate John Adams came sailing into view, bearing certain promotions, one of which constituted Lieutenant Somers as full Commander.

A Naval Exploit of Note

Four attacks were made upon Tripoli, and then Commander Somers persuaded the Commodore to authorize an experiment. A certain ketch, which had been employed in bringing supplies from Malta, was a tender to the fleet. Built originally by the French as a gunboat, in an expedition against Egypt, she had passed into the hands of the Bashaw, and was now a capture of the Americans, who called the little craft the Intrepid.

Commander Somers proposed to fill this craft with powder, load her deck with projectiles, and sail at night into the midst of the Tripolitan fleet and blow the whole collection out of the water.

Elaborate preparations were made. One hundred barrels of powder were poured into a central compartment, fuses and port-fires were carefully arranged, shot and shells were piled above. Lieutenant Henry Wadsworth, of the Constitution, volunteered to go as second in command, and ten brave Yankee seamen made up the crew. Lieutenant Joseph Israel, of the Constitution, joined at the last moment. A couple of boats were taken in tow to provide a possible means of escape.

A Sad but Heroic Ending   The entire fleet was pervaded with a tense feeling of sadness and admiration for the little group of venturers which reported upon the Intrepid at 8 P. M., September 4, 1804. An hour later anchor was up and the sails trimmed for the narrow gap in the reefs several miles away. The long line of ships was peopled with the silent spectators of this fearful undertaking.

A long hour elapsed, and then those who had marine glasses saw the flicker of a lantern far away across the breakers, and a moment later a great gleam of light, flecked with flying wreckage, and finally a "sound like thunder," the bursting of shells, and the silence which closed over a failure which, perhaps, meant death.

And all night long the crews watched for the coming of the boats and the cheery shouts of the seamen, but when daylight spread abroad, there was no dot upon the heaving reach in front, only the surf, and behind it the gloomy castle, the low town and the scattered huts of the fishermen, with the gunboats of the pirate huddled together like frightened ducks.

But over upon the shore that morning, Captain Bainbridge and Surgeon Cowdery, of the Philadelphia, found the fragments of the Constitution's cutter, and as the bodies came in upon the tide, blackened and torn, they were buried in the sands, the officers a little aside, and there ended the story of Somers, of Somers' Point, leaving a legacy to the navy in the mystery of that night, which is still talked about in the mess-rooms of the American warsmen; and just why the Intrepid was prematurely exploded has never been settled; but old Commodore Preble used to say that Somers had sworn that the Bashaw should not get the powder, and that when he had run upon a reef in the darkness, he lighted the fuse, and in the turmoil of waters failed to get away. And this is just what the fleet all agreed upon, considering how well they knew Somers.

The Gallant Hobson

Since this record was penned another boy-hero has impressed his name upon the enduring pages of our naval history, wonderfully similar in its situations with the incident of Tripoli. The entrance into the harbor of Santiago and sinking the Merrimac by Ensign Hobson and his men has fortunately had a more happy denoue- ment. In considering the noteworthy record of the old Somers family, one is led to the supposition that their strain is likely to spring from the same brave stock as that of the heroic but unfortunate Sir George Somers, Kt., who perished by the loss of his ship upon the reefs of the Bermudas in the year 1609, while upon the way to the relief of the starving colonists upon the Virginia plantations. Every visitor to Bermuda will recall the monument to his honor in the wall of the Public Garden of quaint old St. George's, which was named for him.

St. George's Bermuda

A pioneering people, located upon the sea-coast, with a broad reach of tide-washed meadow in front, protected from the open ocean by almost continuous ramparts of sand; an arable border of land between this and the inland wilderness, from which comes the out-flow of navigable streams, possess, at their command, a wide variety of profitable pursuits. Their different occupations, in the forest, upon the sea, or in the less hazardous tillage of the soil, tending to the development of a hardy ancestry, fit to found a thrifty and deeply rooted native population.

People of the Coast

These forefathers of the modern New Jerseyman of this section, were equally farmers, wood-choppers, shipbuilders, hunters, traders and sailors. The fine, cultivated lands, which now reach down to the fragrant salt marsh, through which the old road along the coast has its way, were cleared by them. Many a fine craft has slid from its cradle here, and gone out upon the deep, manned by the sons of Absecon, whose schooling in the coastwise trade has made them valuable in our navy when our wars have called them forth. Saw mills were plentiful in the old days, and salt works were scattered upon the islands. Probably one of the most attractive and remunerative trades was that of the hunter and fishermen, for the woods were full of the game commonly found in this latitude, including the bear, panther and deer, the pheasant, wild turkey, wild pigeon, partridge and woodcock, and, in the marshes, the wild goose and the duck. The thoroughfares were alive with sheepshead, rock, sea bass, flounders and perch, and the getting of subsistence was an easy thing to do. The Indian word, *Absecon*, is said to signify " The Place of Swans."

A Legend Tradition, often cruel and unjust, declares that the business of the wrecker was an active pursuit along this coast. No doubt the flotsam and jetsam of the sea brought its share to the substance of the people, and lent an element of excitement to the secluded existence of the natives, which gave it welcome zest.

A curious suggestion of the cost of wayfaring in the Jerseys in the last century is gained from an old tariff of prices enacted by the County of Gloucester for the better regulation of hotels and inns. It is worth some sample quotations:

Every pint of Madeira Wine	1 s. o d.
Every quart Bowl of Punch made of Loaf Sugar and fresh Limes	1 s. 6 d.
Every quart of Mirabo made of Muscovado Sugar	o s. 8 d.
Every quart of Metheglin	1 s. o d.
Every quart of Cyder Royal	o s. 8 d.
Every jill of Brandy	o s. 6 d.
Every jill of Rum	o s. 3 d.
Every Breakfast of Tea, Coffee or Chocolate	o s. 8 d.
Every Breakfast of other victuals	o s. 6 d.
Every hot Dinner or Supper provided for one person, with a pint of Strong Beer or Cyder	1 s. o d.
Every Night's Lodging, each person	o s. 3 d.

The Drinks of Our Forefathers

Atlantic County finally came into being as a distinct political division in the year 1837, and this event may be taken as the mile-stone marking the beginning of the modern order of things. May's Landing became, and still continues to be, the County seat.

A Shore County   Atlantic County now embraces the townships of Mullicas, Buena Vista, Hamilton, Galloway, Weymouth, and Egg Harbor. It forms an irregular quadrangle, having upon its southeastern side a sea front of twenty miles. Mullicas, or Little Egg Harbor River, and Tuckahoe River are respectively, its northeastern and southwestern limits.

Long Branch was locally noted as a seaside resort soon after the close of the Revolutionary War. Sixty years ago three hotels of considerable proportions were there maintained and a steamboat plied to and from the Amboys regularly.

The statement is made that Reuben Tucker opened the first beach hotel along the middle coast upon Short or Tucker's Beach. It is referred to in *Watson's Annals*. This house was burned about fifty years ago. John Horner, who kept the Tucker hotel above mentioned for a time, built a small house at the southern end of Long Beach about 1815. It was bought by a party of Philadelphians in 1822 and after being enlarged was called the Philadelphia Company House. It was near the once famous and popular "Bonds," built in 1847.

In the middle of the present century Cape May was already an old time resort, popular especially with the affluent families of the South, but the region of Absecon was less understood by the average resident of Philadelphia than is the coast of Oregon to-day. Only the tireless occasional gunner toiled along the dusty miles of the winding roads through the jungles of pine to tramp across its marshes and sand dunes. Extending along the margin of the dry plateau bordering the lonely meadows was the Old Shore Road with its scattered hamlets and intermediate farms of the amphibious native Jerseymen, a class equally at home at the plow and the tiller. Over upon the dreary waste of Absecon Beach, where no beacon light yet warned the sailor from its outer shoals, was the ruin of the salt works of the first inhabitant, Jeremiah Leeds, an officer in the Revolutionary Army, who located here in 1785. The Steelman and Chamberlain families were also owners of beach property here. The whole stretch of beach, as level and broad as it exists to-day, was associated in the minds of the mainlanders only in connection with its tragic chronicle of wrecks.

First Hotels

"THE DREARY WASTE OF ABSECON BEACH"

Atlantic City.   Chapter 11.

The traveler seaward bound to Atlantic City gains his first appetizing whiff of the savory odor wafted from the wide expanse of salt meadow at Pleasantville. As the train halts here for a moment he may note that it is a scattering village of undefined extent wherein the old houses, built long before Atlantic City came into existence, lurk beneath the shadows of large trees, and new ones stand out in the glory of this season's paint in the full sunshine.

The Old Shore Road

It will be seen, too, that a well-graded road traverses the place parallel with the edge of the land, which is, indeed, the principal thoroughfare of the village. This is the Old Shore road, extending from Leeds Point at the north to Somers Point upon the south, and passing through the intermediate settlements of Oceanville, Absecon, Cottage Hill, Pleasantville, Bakerstown, Linwood and Bethel.

This road and its characteristic environment have been but little changed by the vast increase in population and values over upon the immediate sea front. For many generations it has been the highway binding together the continuous farms of the amphibious natives. Between Pleasantville and Somers Point it has lost much of its traffic since the building of the branch railroad to the latter haven.

An Early Type

The early families of the region, whose fathers, sons and brothers found profit upon both the

A TYPICAL OLD SHORE HOME

sea and the land, held broad farms extending from the tidewater thoroughfares over the meadow and far back across the ridge into the pine barrens to the westward. The ridge land, with an average elevation of from 25 to 30 feet above high tide, proved an ideal trucking strip. The heirs of each generation divided their inherited lands, each retaining a portion of the meadow, field and woodland, the present holdings being often ribbon-like strips, like the ancient seigniories of the Beauport Road, below Quebec, and thus numerous branches of the Somers, Steelman, Scull, English, Ireland, Adams, Ryan and Lake families are scattered along the Old Shore Road.

Natives Inland The highway skirts the margin of the upland, affording almost continuous outlooks across the meadows to Longport, Brigantine Beach, Atlantic City, Ocean City and Beasley's Point. The white pleasure fleets are seen cruising in and about the inlets. Forty or fifty years ago the mainlanders were the guardians of the coast, and at the first sight of naked spars projected above the sand-dunes or of black hulls lashed by the surf, they swarmed tumultuously across the wet marshes to gather the flotsam and jetsam of somebody's misfortune. Nowadays the Jersey coaster of Atlantic County goes over to the shore in frequent local trains to jostle awhile in vanity fair, or, perhaps, drives over in the moist dawn his load of "garden sass" for the certain and profitable market that awaits him there. A good **Quiet Highways** turnpike road makes this an easy expedition. Much of the table supplies of the great resort is grown along the Old Shore Road, and it's worth a day's drive to see the thrifty expanses of all the seasonable fruits and vegetables, not to mention the quaint old gardens, flower beds and wide-spreading trees that rally around the gray mansions built by Jersey skippers long, long ago.

My friend J—— is a business man in Philadelphia. Being an expert in his occupation, his business can be led. Therefore, for five months in the year he leaves his city home and takes a little farm of a dozen acres, with a comfortable house, close beside the Old Shore Road. Here, with his family, he dwells all summer, working at his table, "bossing" the man who tills the farm on shares, fishing, and, with the rest of his brood, growing brown and impervious to the able-bodied mosquitoes that, it must be confessed, do inhabit this latitude.

Jersey Arcadia To enter for a day or so into the simplicity of this Arcadia I left the cars at Bakersville. We first went to the post-office, the social rallying point of the little place.

To gauge a country village one must go to the post-office, and the cemetery. At the Bakersville Post-office were gathered sundry old captains, Cap'n Bob, Cap'n Tom and Cap'n Jack, hearty, ruddy old fellows, rejoicing, most of them, in the fruits of many long cruises, full of narrative as the Ancient Mariner, and not altogether reconciled to the sort of innovation represented by the pretty city girls, halting in their dog cart for the mail to be sorted. The inherent provincialism of many of these old residents is found in the candle-mold still used in many of the farm-houses.

The Old Shore Road is hard and level, a real joy to the cyclers that spin to and from Somers Point. Its picturesque suggestion is almost constant, needing only an English to find and paint its gnarled cedars, willows and oaks; its rounded maples, hickories and walnuts and all its confusion of underbrush. There are several old farmyards along the way, choked with sea junk of all sorts. Some gray-tinted readers will recall, doubtless, **Along the Road** the old-time Dolphin Hotel, at Somers Point, with the cedar grove upon the slope. Probably the new hotels clustered beyond have lured away some of its trade, but it still continues business cheerfully "at the old stand." About a mile back from the road, near Linwood, is the practically abandoned village of Bargaintown. Probably the colonists there got more than they bargained for.

In the matter of theology the Baptists have got a clear lead, and are away to the windward along the Old Shore Road. Upon a Sunday the way is bright with pilgrims to the frequent chapels, but the unregenerate also

31

throng the road in vehicles of all degrees. Upon Sunday it is pleasant to loiter down one of the lanes that end at a wharf redolent with oystering, where fleets of schooners lay at anchor for want of profitable occupation. Cat-boats skim before the breeze, and fiddler crabs spatter in regiments through the ooze at one's feet, and sitting there one may muse and wonder why the world at large should worry itself so grievously when so much plenty can be found by looking for it, and why Philadelphians should broil in narrow streets when, for so little, they might have farms somewhere hereabout, and wear out last year's coats and dresses in reasonable peace and comfort.

There is but one single shadow athwart this idyllic scene. It is in the danger that the Old Shore Road will become fashionable. Already the Country Club of Atlantic City, duly mentioned elsewhere, has taken to itself an old time farm-house and a wide reach of land between the old highway and the sedge, and now the red coats of the ardent golfers fleck the scene so lately the undisturbed domain of the ruminative cow. The restless capitalist is turning his speculative eye hitherward, and it may be that the year is in sight when the Old Shore Road in its quaintness and simplicity will become a boulevard of modern estates, its peculiar charm for the lover of nature existing only as a fading memory of the days that were.

Atlantic City.   Chapter III.

To Dr. Jonathan Pitney, a progressive resident of Absecon village, and Samuel Richards, a manufacturer of glass, local history awards the honor of first recognizing the superior possibilities of this place for the development of a resort for people from the cities. A casual study of the map of Central New Jersey affords no special hint of the advantage of this particular stretch of shore above that either to the north or south of it for many miles, save that here only it was possible to build a railroad direct to the beach, and it was to the promotion of this railroad that Dr. Pitney bent his energies. In 1852 when this movement began there were but six houses, small and weatherbeaten, upon the island.

The Birth of a City

That some special reasons do exist which have contributed to the advantage of Atlantic City will appear more fully in later pages. One of

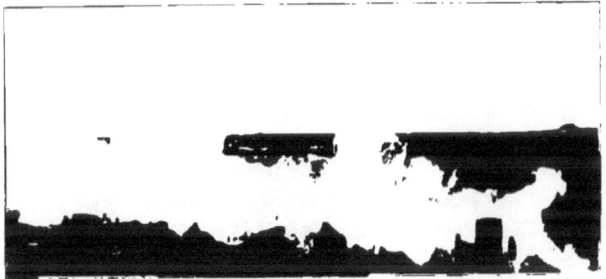

these is the fact that here the line of the shore trends to the westward to a greater degree than at any other portion of the coast, giving an ocean exposure but little removed from southern, which deflects, at a sharp angle, the heavy scour of northeasterly storms. Another and very important condition urged very strenuously by physicians is that Absecon Beach is belted by a broad thoroughfare of pure sea water always running in and out, quite undiluted by fresh water streams and securing perfect immunity from malaria. These and many other advantages were doubtless urged by indomitable Dr. Pitney, and believed by many who listened to his enthusiastic predictions, for, upon June 24, 1852, the subscription books for the stock of the Camden & Atlantic Railroad Company were opened at the Arch Street House in Philadelphia, ten thousand shares were taken and the books were closed the same day. The incorporators were John W. Mickel, Andrew K. Hay, John H. Coffin, John Stanger, Jesse Richards, Thos. H. Richards, Edmund Taylor, Jos. Thompson, Robert B. Risley, Enoch Doughty and Jonathan Pitney. The thirty-eight original stockholders elected the following gentlemen as the first Board of Directors : William Coffin, Joseph Porter, Andrew R. Hay, Thos. H. Richards (who subsequently gave place to J. C. Da Costa), Enoch Doughty, Jonathan Pitney, Stephen Colwell, Samuel Richards and William W. Fleming. The first president was John C. Da Costa.

Early in the movement of this enterprise the projectors were so fortunate as to secure the professional services of Mr. Richard B. Osborne, a young but already well-known civil engineer, whose enthusiasm for the success of what was regarded by many investors as a very hazardous venture, was strong enough to convince doubters, and whose predictions have all been verified a hundred-fold. Mr. Osborne is one of the few survivors of those who "made" Atlantic City, and is still a resident of Philadelphia. He not only surveyed and put into motion the first of the iron bands uniting the Quaker City with the New Jersey coast in this section, but he planned the city of pleasure which was to spring, almost like a scene of magic, from the barren waste of sands upon Absecon Beach. Twenty-five years after the completion of the Camden & Atlantic Railroad, at a great

The Camden &
Atlantic Railroad

quadri-centennial of the event held at Atlantic City in June, 1879, Mr. Osborne had the happiness to see the verification of his forecasts and as one of the principal speakers of the occasion to furnish an accurate history of the inception, completion and operation of the original railroad, which, as reprinted, in part, in this book will have an increasing value as an authoritative chapter of reference.

Mr. Osborne first referred to the great difficulties encountered in enlisting interest in the project, and to his first interview with the officials upon May 24, 1852, and then continued: "Arrangements were made on that day with me for a preliminary survey. Accordingly, in this very month of June, seven-and-twenty years ago, my engineers, under the active supervision of the late Mr. E. Lyons, as my principal assistant engineer, stretched rapidly across the State of New Jersey the thread of our first experimental line, which afterwards was woven into an iron band $59\frac{7}{10}$ miles long, to bind Camden and Philadelphia to this beach.

"This survey was completed to the sea on the 18th of June, 1852, and the engineering party became that day the first bathers that had traveled along the line of the Camden & Atlantic Railroad to get a reviving plunge in the waters of the Atlantic, an example which it has rejoiced millions since to be able to follow.

RICHARD B. OSBORNE, C. E.

"The report of this survey was submitted by me to the directors on the 21st of June, 1852, who at once adopted it. Previous to the completion of the experimental survey, the directors, by the solicitation and the request of their engineer, made a carriage trip across the State to visit the Island and Absecon Beach, and pass their opinion on there being a fitting site there

PRIMEVAL
SOLITUDES OF
ABSECON
BEACH

'for a bathing village,' to be called Absecon, as its beach bore that name. We had a weary journey through the deep, dry sand, and after leaving the village of Long a-coming (now the town of Berlin—the name Long-a-coming seemed appropriate for all the country we passed through), we at length gained the village of Absecon, and were joined by the directors, Messrs. Pitney and Doughty.

"The flat, wet marshes, with their water ditches and thoroughfares, turned our party into a sail-boat, by way of Absecon Bay, landing us at the point on the Inlet now occupied by the Inlet Pavilion. The island appeared most certainly uninviting to the eyes of city gentlemen, and its sterile sand heaps, naked in their desolation, gave it a weird, wild look, a veritable desert without a building on it that many would deem worthy of being called a habitation. My directors, save Messrs. Pitney and Doughty, were disappointed: they did not deem it desirable as a site for the proposed bathing village, that to build a railroad to reach such a wild spot would be a reckless piece of adventure. All of these gentlemen were doubtful about the possibility of a locomotive being sustained while crossing these meadows, some of them felt certain this never could be accomplished. Thus, indeed, all hope of making our trip and visit the means of leaving a favorable impression on the minds of these gentlemen, as to the feasibility of the project, and of giving them any sure hope of a return, and of getting from them a decision that would settle the question of the construction of work that in the opinion of the engineer was certain to prove a boon and blessing to the city of Philadelphia, to carry civilization and wealth to that part of the State within reach of its influence, and to yield a rich reward to its enterprising promoters, seemed almost lost.

A Gloomy
Prospect

"It was the turning point on which everything depended. There were no like interests elsewhere to be secured that would offer sufficient inducements to attempt it. The words and wills of those few gentlemen in that short hour, on that memorable day, controlled events measured by millions. I heard their expressions of disappointment and disapprobation with regret. In reply I said : Gentlemen, every objection made (if viewed properly) is really an argument in its favor. I pleaded for the site, and in this Messrs. Pitney and Doughty coincided with me ; I showed that its rough, wild state was precisely what would give them the control of the ground at low rates, and that here was a fortune in itself. This argument was very assuring to the directors, 'if only the meadows could be crossed by the trains.' I was not unprepared to meet this question, and for the time settled it in the minds of the gentlemen by giving them a guarantee that the locomotive should pass safely over its whole extent. **When Speech was Golden**

"I quote from a communication written in June, 1852, to show how this assurance was imparted and the efforts that were necessary to remove the doubts occasioned by the first visit of the directors to this beach just described, viz.: 'As the pioneers through this country in railroad works, you will surely be the recipients of large profits—yes, much larger than can accrue to many roads which traverse a country intersected with railroad lines.' Again, 'Your road will have the benefit of all the latest improvements, and if the public be not excluded from a fair participation in them, it must prove a popular work, affording the largest accommodation at the least cost.' Again, 'I will assume that but 20,000 of the inhabitants of Philadelphia will, in the first year, be attracted to your road, while the Cape May visitors last season numbered 120,000. Twenty thousand passengers will thus be taken on your railway, and freight and other articles in like proportion. There has been enough evidence given you by me to show that in all my estimates I have kept far within the bounds of what I should be justified in going to.'

"When the report of the experimental survey was adopted by the Board on the 21st of June instructions were also given to proceed with the final location of the road, and accordingly, on the 1st of July, 1852, my engineering parties took the field, and the 'location' of the line to the sea was completed, and the estimate made by the 25th of August following, and on this date, also, John C. Da Costa, at the earnest solicitation of myself, after he had declined to accept the position, consented to act and was elected president of the Company.

The Opening Wedge

"On the 31st of August, 1852, I submitted to my Board proposals for the construction of the whole road, based on my estimated fixed rates per mile ; and on the first of September, 1852, those proposals were accepted, subject to certain changes of the line to accommodate the Waterford manufactories and Spring Garden, and subject, also, to other requirements, all of which were not completed till after the contract was signed on the 4th of March, 1853. This change was a detour that shortened my long tangent some 10 miles and left only the present straight line of 25 continuous miles.

"On the 2d of September, 1852, the construction work of the road was sub-let to Mr. P. O'Reilly, and he received his first bid from sub-contractors, for sections of one mile each, on the 4th of September, 1852.

"There was no formal breaking ground ; the contractors were set to work as soon as their houses could be erected, and in September, 1852, the construction by grading was started.

"The first estimate, returned December, 1852, was for work on eight sections between sections 4 and 32 and amounted to a payment of $10,000.

"The crossing of the Camden and Amboy rails at Camden by those of this road was laid by night in the month of July, 1853.

"On the 20th of June, 1853, the whole management of the contract work was given up by Mr. O'Reilly to Mr. John H. Osborne, Civil Engineer and previously manager of the Richmond and Danville Railroad, who completed the three-fourths of the whole contract that had not been touched.

On the 11th of September of the same year this gentleman was also chosen by the directors as their Resident Engineer for the benefit of his advice and for the more active management and superintendence on their behalf of the progress of the work, and for the return of the estimates.

"Track was laid on the road between Camden and Haddonfield, and also at Absecon during August, 1853. Passenger trains commenced running from Camden to Haddonfield in August, 1853, and to Winslow, 27 miles, regularly in January, '54. The wharves at this date at Camden and the station grounds there were nearly complete. In February, 1854, a high storm tide was driven across the meadows and damaged the grading of the road-bed; and on the 16th of April following, after the work had been replaced, a northeast storm and spring tide made a clean sweep of the same work. This class of road-bed was then abandoned and the track was laid on the original sod, except at the thoroughfares, where it has rested in spite of storm and flood for five and twenty years. It is right to say the railroad company bore the whole expense of the third renewal. It has made good the guarantee given by the engineer to his directors in 1852, and the locomotives make their trips now at their usual speed. The whole work was completed in time for the opening celebration.

"On July 1st, 1854, the pioneer excursion train stood at the platform in Camden and steamed forth its greeting to 600 guests—gentlemen of the press from New York and Philadelphia, and friends from town and country, who had assembled to celebrate the completion of the line that had occupied two and twenty months in building the 58_{10}^{3} miles of main road. Its opening to public travel was on July 4, 1854."

The First Through Train

The excursion train conveying the six hundred guests was composed of nine long cars. The "Atsion" engine was selected for the trip. At Waterford, the residence of Judge Porter, one of the directors and early friends of the road, a salute of artillery greeted the arrival. Conspicuous was also a large wreath of native Jersey laurels, and wrought in the interior

Through by Rail of it the words in flowers, "Welcome to Waterford." It was a poetic emblem of the faith of the man which had always encircled and wreathed around the enterprise.

From Waterford the train, which left Camden at 9.30 A. M., then started for the embryonic Atlantic City. It was the first engine with passenger train that passed over the entire road, and it reached the United States Hotel by 12 M., thus with all the stops at the various stations to respond to the earnest congratulations of friends.

At the meeting of the guests of the railroad company in the great saloon of the United States Hotel spirited addresses were made after the dinner cloth had been removed, Mr. T. H. Dudley moving for an organization of the meeting by the calling of Judge Grier to the chair, and who appointed the vice-presidents, among whom were Henry C. Carey, Hon. Abraham Browning, J. C. TenEyck, T. P. Carpenter, Robert Morris and many other gentlemen of note were among the vice-presidents. The first impressive address was made by Henry C. Carey, who offered also an appreciative resolution, which was seconded by Mr. Browning in an eloquent speech. These were followed by addresses from J. C. TenEyck, Gen. Wyncoop, President John C. DaCosta, Mr. Montgomery and Judge Grier.

The train containing the guests left Atlantic City between 5 and 6 P. M., and arrived safely at Camden about 8 P. M.

Success Assured   The success of the road, the Board now felt, was assured. A new era was opened for New Jersey, and the engineer had time to congratulate himself that his plans had been perfected and his promises made good thus far.

"The line of the road along which the locomotive brought us to-day was located on the 20th day of August, 1852. Surveys of the beach and island had been made by my principal assistant, M. E. Lyons, and also by Messrs. Rowland and Clement, but these last were of later date.

"The centre line of the railroad was run parallel to the general line of the beach for a distance from the inlet southward, of over two and a quarter miles, for the purpose of fixing a line that would be suitable for a base on which to plan the village, and which would permit the streets to be carried on in their proper directions whenever requisite to enlarge the village plot. On this as a base, December, 1852, under the instructions of the directors, I proceeded to lay out the plot of the proposed Bathing Village. This plan was completed and submitted to a full board in the middle of January, 1853.

"There is, says an old proverb, 'Nothing in a name.' As the engineer I denied that it was applicable to this case, and when, before my Board, I unrolled a great and well-finished map of the proposed new bathing place, they saw in large letters of gold, stretching over the waves that were delineated thereon as breaking on Absecon beach the words, 'Atlantic City.' This title was at once approved of by the Board. It was unanimously adopted, and Atlantic City that day came into existence, on paper, and in thirteen and a half months afterward, viz., on the third of March, 1854, was created, by act of incorporation, a city in reality. I have ever claimed, and do so now, that this name created in the minds of men throughout the Union a certain interest in this city, and this interest it was sought to further secure by giving to each State its own avenue, and hence the name of every State from Maine to Iowa to-day designates the avenues that run east and west, while the general parallelism of the shore of the Atlantic with the main line for 2.3 miles suggested the names of all the great oceans of the world for the avenues running north and south.

The Survey and Naming of Atlantic City

"It is true, then, that there is something in a name, and I may be permitted, without egotism, to say that I am proud of having christened her and her avenues and stamped on her a dignity that my old departed friends, Messrs. Pitney and Doughty, little dreamed of when they talked together on the scheme of getting up a 'bathing village,' to be called Absecon.

"Early in February, 1853, after the plan of this city had been adopted by the Board, a committee was sent down to Absecon Island, composed of Dr. Jonathan Pitney, a director, and Robert Frazer, the faithful and efficient secretary and treasurer of the Company. Dr. Pitney was acquainted with the Messrs. Cordery, Adams, Paterson, Bartlett, Carter, Read, Bowe, and other landowners on the Island. Mr. Robert Frazer took with him a draft of the plot of the new city. These gentlemen were instructed to confer with the owners, (who had been notified December 11, '52, that commissioners would be appointed to assess the damages. This land was bought for less than $20 per acre ; it brings to-day in the central parts $50 a foot)— and obtain possession of the land for the formation of the roadbed on Atlantic avenue, arranged on the plot to be the great *Highway* for the accommodation of the main tracks of the railway.

"The tracklaying commenced May 29th, 1854, and enough for the immediate wants of the road, after its opening from about one-quarter of a mile above the United States Hotel, was finished by the last of June, 1854.

"Such was the barren condition of the Island, that on the first visit of the engineering party, on the 14th of June, 1852, they were unable to get anything to eat ; and Mr. Stack wrote, even on the 4th of June, 1853, that he could get some board for the sub-contractor's hands on the Island, but that he must provide for them tents for their shelter.

An Early Impression

"I remember clearly the misery of my first visit with the engineering party. The Island was rough and sterile, producing only rushes and stunted brush, though in spots the magnolia was to be found. It was comfortless to the weary traveler. There was no accommodation for our little party. But there was faith in the future ; experience of what had been achieved elsewhere under some similar conditions, determination to persevere, and a power to foresee the great revolution that would be produced by even a moderate success.

"This is the picture of the early beginnings of this city. The present reality is all around you and speaks loudly for itself ; yet to enable others to join you in the contrast, I will say a few words about the glory in which the city of Atlantic stands clothed to-day.

A "CROWDED BEACH" IN THE EARLY DAYS

"Connected as I have been with the laying out of towns and cities in the Western States, and professionally engaged in Chicago at the time when her population was less than 5000, and when the great influx of our eastern men began and large investments were made, I was carried along on the tide and became, professionally, the means of placing many towns and paper cities profitably on the market. I know but one of them, to-day, that has not made its mark; but few of them, in twenty-five years, can show a better record than Atlantic City. My report of August, 1852, foretold much of it all, and the statements therein were then considered enthusiastic, but she has, in some things, exceeded even my sanguine hopes. She has made herself more widely known than many towns and cities twice her age. She stands to-day a grand example of the power of a first-class railroad to achieve wonders that wise men once thought chimerical. Her churches, numbering one dozen; her schools, where over 1,000 children are instructed; her five or six beneficial societies; her daily mail and daily newspaper; her five trains a day from the city of Philadelphia; her passenger horse-cars, which of course every important city must now have; her lighthouse, built twenty-two years ago; her signal service station, city hall, jail, and fire department; her fifty hotels, many of which are first-class; her numerous beautiful villas, that appreciative gentlemen, bankers, merchants, physicians

In 1879

and professional men own and occupy; her hundreds of cottages; her boarding houses; her 34,000 inhabitants, during her busy season; her 4000 permanent residents, and the fact that about five and a-half millions of people have enjoyed her invigorating and health-giving climate, and her numerous inviting recreations on land and sea since she was opened for the public good. All these form a picture so full of interest, so rich in all the bright tints of a glorious reality in the foreground, that the original background has almost faded away, and had to be repainted to give our visitors to Atlantic City some slight idea of the real contrast.

"There is another point particularly worthy of mention, viz.: the wonderful effect a residence here has on invalids. This is testified to by scores of medical men, who send their patients to the sea as the best prescription they can bestow on them. It is testified to by the multitudes who have received the benefits.

Nature's Great Physician

"In 1852 I called Atlantic City 'the lungs of Philadelphia,' through which she would inhale much of the health and ability of body and mind that now characterizes her business and professional men; and she has proved the truth of the assertion."

Mr. Osborne referred to Mr. Robert Frazer, the first secretary and treasurer of the Camden & Atlantic Railroad, to Mr. John H. Osborne, who became the superintendent in 1855, Mr. George W. Richards, the second president, Mr. John Tucker, Mr. John Lucas, Mr. D. H. Mundy, and others identified with the early years of the Company. He predicted with remarkable accuracy many of the great things which have since become realities and urged the importance of moving to secure government aid in creating at the inlet a great port of entry. Mr. Richard B. Osborne is a native of England. His early engineering experiences were largely under the guidance of the late Moncure Robinson, C. E. He has long been identified with many of the most important railroad, canal and municipal engineering achievements of his time.

Atlantic City. Chapter IV.

Upon the legal creation of Atlantic City, Chalkley S. Leeds, a son of one of the original owners, became the first mayor and his brother, Robert B. Leeds, was the first city treasurer.

First Administration

It was, perhaps, believed by the originators of the young city that the supply of States would always afford a sufficiency of names for the transverse avenues placed upon the city plan, but the latest official map gives us a long list of new streets to the west of Chelsea bearing the titles of American cities. At Boston avenue, down by the old Sea View Excursion House, Atlantic avenue comes to the sea front and Pacific avenue is halted in its course, a matter somewhat confusing to the stranger.

The hotel man who had ventured thirty years ago to announce his intention to keep open house all winter would have been esteemed a visionary unfit for the practical duties of a Boniface. In 1868 the average attendance at the schools was 110 pupils. Thirty thousand dollars was expended upon educational facilities.

At that time the best known hotels were the United States (famous for its fine park), where the first train load of excursionists dined

Early Hotels of Atlantic City

when the railroad was opened, Congress Hall, Mansion House and Surf House. Other hotels and cottages which were all well filled in the summer were these: Neptune House, Light House Cottage, Alhambra, White House, Seaside House, Clarendon House, Ashland House, Glen's Inlet House, Kentucky House, Chester County House, Bedloe's (built in 1854), Pennsylvania Cottage, Cottage Retreat (built in 1854), Macy House, Reed House, Arch Street House, Constitution House, West Philadelphia House, Bradley House, Sherman House, Excursion House, Grove Cottage, Columbia Cottage, Sand House and Atlantic House.

Besides these were scores of less pretentious boarding places scattered through the young city. At this time the road across the marsh, bridging the thoroughfare, was being developed.

The Atlantic House, which originally stood at Baltic and Florida avenues was in its original state a tavern for oystermen, kept by Mrs. Leeds. It was built about 1812 and is the oldest building now upon the island. It now stands on Baltic avenue near Massachusetts avenue.

The heavy travel over the Camden & Atlantic Railroad in the Centennial year, together with the rapid progress of the young city led to the incorporation of the Philadelphia & Atlantic Railroad Company, which was formerly narrow gauge but changed to standard gauge in 1884, now operated by the Philadelphia & Reading Railway Company. This line opened for business June 25, 1877. The resulting competition proved of the greatest benefit to Atlantic City, both in the reduction of fares and freight as well as an increase in the number of trains, especially in summer, and a decidedly more rapid schedule. "The Reading" route was double tracked in 1889.

Railroad Progress

In the year 1880 a third bond of iron was extended between Philadelphia and the sea through an extension of a branch from the West Jersey Railroad, known as the West Jersey & Seashore Railroad, which also affords through service without change between New York and Atlantic City.

Upon the acquisition of the Camden & Atlantic Railroad by the Pennsylvania Railroad Company the old name disappeared and it became the Atlantic City Division of the Pennsylvania Railroad. On completion of the great bridge over the Delaware River above the city in the spring of 1896, with its incidental trackage, which joins the old line at Haddonfield, the Pennsylvania Railroad Company began to run its fast trains to the shore from Broad street station. This line, which is double tracked, has been laid in the past winter with " 100 lb." steel rails. The proposed terminal station at Atlantic City will be upon a scale of magnificence unknown at any resort in the world. The Present Era

The West Jersey & Seashore Railroad is largely devoted to way trains and local traffic. It is expected that its tracks will be elevated through Camden, and other important improvements made in the near future.

The old Philadelphia & Atlantic City Narrow Gauge Railroad was acquired by the Philadelphia and Reading Railway Company in 1885, and soon afterward was practically reconstructed upon standard gauge lines. Under its modern title of "Atlantic City Railroad," it has always enjoyed a heavy traffic in pleasure and business travel. With ferry-boats from both Chestnut and South streets to its terminal opposite the foot of Washington avenue, it maintains a rapid service upon double tracks; dividing the honors with the Pennsylvania Railroad in giving a service to and from the shore unequalled by that of any other resort.

A Noted Comfort   A recent number of the *Scientific American* contains the statement, that the Atlantic City trains are the fastest in the world; but so smooth is the trackage and fine the equipment that, although running at a mile per minute, the superior speed is not noticeable, except in the fact that while absorbed in a brief story upon the pages of a magazine, the traveler leaves and arrives.

The once ubiquitous "duster" has long since become obsolete, and the excursionist alights at the terminal quite unsoiled by the slightest evidence of travel.

BEACH LOOKING WEST

The new Pennsylvania Ferryhouse, at the foot of Market street, Philadelphia, has been recently completed. It is a modern two story building, which is an ornament to Philadelphia's water-front.

At the foot of Chestnut street, the "Reading" has also built its Ferry terminal at large expense. These improvements, with double-decked boats, will make travel to the shore still more popular than heretofore.

A sketch made by the writer twenty-five years ago from the lighthouse, recalls to mind most vividly the relative paucity of Atlantic City's attractions, and the comparatively limited area covered by the town in 1873. At the Inlet, a single small open pavilion of one story stood upon the site of the present large structure, a rather shaky pier reaching out into the Thoroughfare for the accommodation of the little fleet of yachts, some of them famous flyers, which afforded one of the chief means of pleasure at the command of the visitor. A horse car line connected the Inlet with the town, over a long stretch of open sand reach.

Atlantic City 25 Years Ago

A few more or less pretentious hotels had been built upon the seaward side of Pacific avenue. Narrow and precarious plank-walks extended outward, here and there, toward the beach, subject to the vicissitudes of winter gales and high tides, elements which played havoc frequently with the long rank of gay little pavilions which bravely faced

PENNSYLVANIA R. R. TERMINAL, ATLANTIC CITY

PHILADELPHIA AND ATLANTIC CITY R. R. TERMINAL, READING ROUTE, ATLANTIC CITY

the surf and furnished bathing facilities then regarded as more than ample for the present and future.

Heston's very complete Atlantic City Guide Book states, that the first bath-house upon the beach was built by Joshua Note, from an old wreck, and at that time there were to be seen upon the beach some fourteen wrecks.

Nearly all of the popular hotels were located between Atlantic and Pacific avenues. The former was fairly lined, upon the shoreward or northern side with structures, some of these still existing, but the majority of which have long since disappeared to make room for more costly and elaborate buildings. Beyond this, all of the flat land between the town and the thoroughfare was unoccupied, save by the embankment of the Camden and Atlantic Railroad, around the terminus of which, Schauffler's and a few smaller houses of entertainment were located.

Happy Days Over at the bridge which carried the road across the thoroughfare toward Pleasantville, the Island House stood, just beyond the present junction of Baltic and Florida avenues, its nearest neighbor being the Higbee House, just built by Jonas Higbee, upon the northward side of the railroad track. What pleasant memories of happy times that name invokes! Jonas Higbee was a rugged manly specimen of the old type of New Jersey coastmen. For many years he was in the employ of the Camden & Atlantic Railroad Company, having charge of the drawbridge at that point. The original Higbee homestead, a little modest building out upon the lonely meadow to the south of the railroad track, was presided over by Mrs. Higbee, a famous cook, in whose cosy little dining room, the hungry members of the Higbee Club were wont to gather, with joyful anticipations, **The Higbee Club** upon Saturdays and Sundays, when they used to come hastening down from the hot city to this pleasant haven with due certainty. The Higbee Club bunked in a little shanty at the southern end of the bridge, the vibrations of which used to shake the tired fishers out of bed in the night when casual freight trains rumbled past, and sometimes, when the tide was high, seemed likely to carry the occupants out to sea while they slept. The rotund Secretary of the Club, a well-known dentist of Philadelphia, kept the log book and nothing counted but sheepshead. A brace of these gamy fellows were esteemed a fair return for a long day of patient effort, beginning with the first indications of rosy dawn, and only ending when night and hunger impelled the fishermen to pull back to the drawbridge, with the prospects of a savory supper to cheer them. The writer recalls one amphibious old native who haunted the thoroughfare with his leaky punt and maintained, it was said,

a multitudinous family somewhere in the depths of the pine scrub, from the products of the waters and the marsh. For a long time this quaint, frowsy old salt enjoyed a monopoly, for he knew, when nobody else could find a nibble, just where the elusive sheepshead were loafing about at any turn of the tide, and the man who was lucky enough to negotiate his valuable services was certain to come in with the best and biggest fish.

After the new house was built by the Higbees, as a natural result of their growing fame, spread abroad by the unwise members of the jolly little club, strangers began to come and trench upon the vested rights of the old timers. Somehow, the members sighed for the little low-built cottage which stood reproachful and silent across the railroad. And so with the passing years the hand of time closed its veracious log book, full of the records of joyous days and wonderful piscatorial adventures, and the Higbee Club became but a memory worthy only of passing mention among the flotsam of bygone times.

All of the level stretch of open meadow, between the thoroughfare at the bridge and the city nearly a mile away, which used to rest so still and dark just before the moon began to glow over the twinkling windows to the eastward, and which was so gloriously rich in color when the early sun poured down upon it, is now covered with a close huddle of houses, not particularly pleasing to the eye, either in architecture or environment.

"MAKING" OF
THE BEACH

An interesting phenomenon of the ocean front, which has, by the way, been worth millions of dollars to Atlantic City, is seen in the gradual "making" of the beach, which, by the piling of the sands, has gradually forced the surf-line outward and safeguarded the city from inundation, adding at the same time a vast area of most valuable property to the city's plan. In the winter of 1866-7 the storms were unusually severe, and the tide swept in almost to the line of Atlantic avenue. There were many,

The Border of
the Deep

in those days, who predicted that the time would come when the sea would swallow up the whole property of the community, and that Atlantic City would be but a costly and extravagant memory. This prediction has long ago been shown to be fallacious, and has been dismissed from the minds of even the most nervous citizen. Last autumn the town was cut off, for several days, from the world-at-large by remarkably high water, which covered the meadows and railroad tracks, but at no time did the sea, which swayed about the iron pillars of the Boardwalk, threaten more than temporary damage upon the immediate ocean front. The regrading of the tracks across the meadows promises to safeguard the city from any similar experience in the future.

Atlantic City. **Chapter V.**

"Oh weel I mind, oh weel I mind,
Tho' now my locks are snow,
How oft langsyne I sought to find
What made the bellows blow!
How, cuddling on my grannie's knee,
I questioned night and day,
And still the thing that puzzled me
Was, where the wind came frae."

The Restless Sea

ALONG THE OLD BOARDWALK

The man who told his little boy that the ocean was salt because the codfish were so numerous, was a type of the large class of people who are never disposed to take the sea seriously. It is associated in their minds with daily romps in the surf, pleasant little cruises off shore, and gleaming moonlight touching the tips of sleepy rollers, which break with tranquilizing monotony all through the summer night. And yet, what is this vast, implacable, treacherous, beautiful thing which spreads away from our very feet, thousands of level but storm-swept miles, to lands we have never seen ; which hides, far down in its sunless depths, such unknown wonders, such myriad victims of its wrath, such strange creatures and shapes ?

From the north to the south it spreads some 8000 miles. Between Greenland and Norway it is but 800 miles wide. Between the peninsula of Florida and the coast of Morocco, upon the parallel of 30° north latitude, it expands to a breadth of 3600 miles. While a line drawn from Cape St. Roque, Brazil, at 5° south latitude, to the coast of Sierra Leone, would be but 1500 miles long. The ocean voyage from Philadelphia to the British Isles is practically 3000 miles long. Ships going eastward are helped by the Gulf Stream, and in coming west, by keeping well up over the Grand Banks, are speeded by the Polar Current, which sweeps around the southern end of Newfoundland.

Rivers of the Sea

The ocean is full of vast rivers—broad ribbons of water hundreds of miles in width, distinct in color and action. The strange, beneficent phenomenon which we call the "Gulf Stream," sweeps across the Southern Ocean, flows along the South and Central American coasts, curving in conformity to the shore lines, makes the circuit of the Gulf of Mexico and rushing through the narrow outlet between Key West and Cuba, swings northward in a current of about fifty miles per diem; spreading out with the resistance of the cold under streams from the Polar regions, and endowing our latitude with a climate which, without this great natural warm-water heater, would be so unendurable as to probably preclude the occupation of this part of the world by human beings. Even with this moderating agency, ours is a comparatively cold coast, for Atlantic City is about one hundred miles further south than Naples; while Nice, the beautiful semi-tropical winter resort of Southern France, where palm trees nod and thrive in the warm atmosphere, is upon the latitude of Portland, Maine. Let us be thankful for the wonderful blue Gulf Stream, over the western margin of which, far down upon the horizon, we may often see the pearly rampart of clouds.

The temperature of the Gulf Stream opposite the New Jersey coast, in the warmest of its three bands, that nearest the coast, is in winter 70

degrees, in spring 71 degrees, in summer 80 degrees, and in autumn 74 degrees.

The average elevation of the land of this globe is less than one-fifth of a mile, while the average depth of the sea is about two miles. The bulk of all the dry land in the world, when considered in its proportions with the sea, is but one in thirty.

The greatest depth found in the Atlantic Ocean is at a point about one hundred miles north of St. Thomas, W. I., where soundings were made to four and four-tenths miles.

From the interesting pages of Heston's Hand Book of Atlantic City, we are permitted to add to this chapter of ocean lore some further interesting facts.

The curvature of the sea level in one mile is eight inches, in three miles it is six feet, and in five miles about sixteen feet. Therefore, a person of six feet in height, standing upon the Boardwalk, could see an object upon the water at the latter distance. *Facts from Heston's Hand=Book*

Water more than sixty fathoms deep appears blue; shallow waters show green. The waves move forward but the water does not. As the top of the wave moves faster than its base, due to the lesser friction, it presently topples over or breaks; this generally occurring as soon as any shallow or submerged obstruction is encountered.

Sea breezes are caused by the action of the sun upon the air above the land. During the day time, the inland air, receiving more heat than that upon the water, rises, and the cooler sea air rushes in to fill the vacuum. In making arrangements to this effect, nature has placed the residents of Atlantic City under a sense of great obligation.

The action of the sea in its perpetual pounding and scouring of the New Jersey sands, is full of interest. Shores recede and advance. To the south of Barnegat all of the beaches wear away at their northeastern ends, and the inlets work southward; above Barnegat the inlets work to the northward. Old Cranberry and Shrewsbury Inlets, for instance, have worked a mile or more to the northward; while important changes have taken place in the openings and shores to the southward. Long Beach "made" outside of Nickus Beach, and closed up old Little Egg Harbor Inlet so completely, that people could walk across at low tide. New Little Egg Harbor Inlet was formed about 1800, and soon afterward ships drawing twelve feet of water could safely pass in or out.

The northeast end of Absecon Beach is much older than the shore further south. In front of the present city it has changed greatly since the town was founded. Mention has been made of the cutting away toward the lighthouse, but between New Jersey and Florida avenues it has advanced many hundreds of feet. Half a century ago, the surf line was about where Haddon Hall, The Chalfonte, Arlington and Brighton Hotels stand, not more than a block from Pacific avenue.

The relative fineness of the sand upon a beach has much to do with its character for stability or change. When the tides recede, the surface of the sand dries, and, being picked up by the sea-breeze, is whirled landward, sinking into little heaps around every bit of drift or herbage. These form small "leas," which catch still further sand, and soon the coarse salt grass springs up to hold it, and thus the ridges grow. Along the Virginia coast, upon such islands as Broadwater, the ridges, due to the lightness of the sand, have become very high, and are covered with dense thickets. Still further south, at Currituck, North Carolina, the sand-hills reach the greatest height upon the Atlantic seaboard, completely engulfing, upon the landward side, miles of forest and even farm houses.

Hardly less interesting than the sands are the broad marshes formed behind them, plentifully threaded with creeks and "thoroughfares," which connect with the wide reaches of bays. These meadows give excellent grazing to many cattle and teem with wild fowl. A curious phenomenon is seen in the fresh water springs which come to their surface, where the kine and the birds may drink.

The sandy area of Atlantic County is about 4000 acres, and the marsh area 38,000 acres.

A list of the various birds found along the coast, including both those of the forest and aquatic species, gives the names of more than one hundred kinds. The varieties of fish are still more numerous. While the hunting and fishing is not, of course, what it was in the early days, the sportsman of the present and future need never go hungry in the neighborhood of these waters.

A DAY WITH THE BIRDS

Atlantic City.   Chapter VII.

The Boardwalk

The spacious permanent Boardwalk extending along the immediate sea-front for a distance of some twenty-five blocks, and continued many blocks to the westward by a narrow structure, is the glory of the city, and in many respects, its most profitable investment. It is the rialto of the masses, the great social exchange for the multitudes from the scores of large hotels, and the hundreds of lesser establishments and cottages so

THE BATHING HOUR

closely packed upon the costly space stretching shoreward, square upon square. It is a pleasant and astonishing " Vanity Fair," the favorite parade for the young and gay, and the delightful out-of-door sanitarium for the tired and age-worn. It always carries the aspect of festivity, suggesting a panorama of life in all its phases. With every hour of the day, and in every season, every condition of weather its aspects change. From this sun-lit gallery, one may watch the sparkle of the glorious sea in its tender moods, or face the tempest when the billows break and war incessantly beneath the foot. Along its iron rail in the bathing hour of a summer's morning, the people cluster like bees, to watch the other multitudes gathered upon the warm gray sands or splashing in the rollers with all the abandon of children. Upon the outward side all is majesty, breadth and mystery. It is the edge of the world. Upon the other is ranged the thousand and one devices of the trader, a far-stretching chain of temptations,

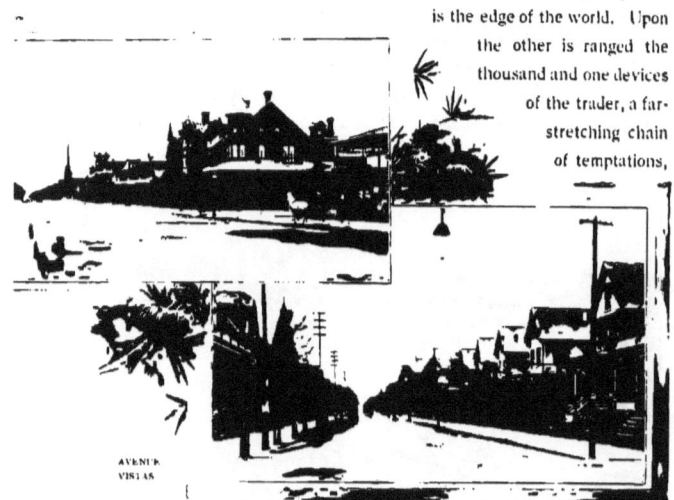

AVENUE VISTAS

every link of which has its own particular form and attraction. It is a gauntlet which few run from end to end, without stopping to pay tribute. Perhaps it would be impossible to accurately estimate the volume of the traffic enjoyed by the owners of these gay pavilions and shops upon Atlantic City's "Midway," but it must run into the hundreds of thousands every year, and the total of rentals when considered might make one dizzy. It is a great object-lesson upon the potency of success. Nearly every human want has its ministers here. Its multitude of signs and banners catch and confuse the eye, the dazzle of the scene banishes every prudent resolve at economy, and so the holiday crowds surge to and fro, in and out of the portals of temples, theatres, casinos, piers and bazaars, scattering the currency of the realm with a reckless prodigality, truly American, and those who spread their wares in the sight of the visitor are rejoiced with prosperity. How barren would be the Boardwalk without its shows and shops, and after all, how much the visitor can get there for the money spent! Many of the stores, notably those dealing in foreign wares, carry superb and costly stocks, fortunes in bric-a-brac. The theatres present excellent entertainments, the merry-go-rounds, the razzle-dazzle, Ferris wheels and temples of mystery, all afford startling sensations, at the smallest possible price of admission, while it is well known that the oriental giants and fat women are quite as ponderous as they are depicted upon the canvas in front of their abiding places, and the anacondas are as ferocious as the most captious could wish. Handsome pavilions, reserved for the guests of the principal hotels, are frequent along the promenade, together with many extensive bathing-houses, enclosing large swimming-tanks, some of which are in use throughout the year.

The Pleasure Piers

Projected from this hurly-burly of pleasure, far out into the surf, are three vast piers upon which are built expansive concert halls, restaurants and pavilions. The most costly and elaborate of these structures, thus daringly built above the restless surge of old ocean, is the one constructed by the Atlantic City Steel Pier Company, at a cost of $200,000. All day long, and far into the night the piers are crowded, the military bands play on, while the summer rolls merrily along.

Boardwalk Glimpses

A tramp along the Boardwalk from the breezy Inlet away down to the old Excursion House is a constitutional. It would more than satisfy the inveterate old sea-dog one always finds among the passengers of

61

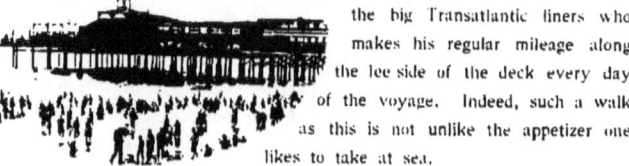 the big Transatlantic liners who makes his regular mileage along the lee side of the deck every day of the voyage. Indeed, such a walk as this is not unlike the appetizer one likes to take at sea.

Up around the Inlet at the eastern extreme of the island, where the white fleets of sloops are always speeding up and down, and where the rollers used to sweep in so perilously close to the big shapely lighthouse, there are acres upon acres of made land, now being rapidly covered by stylish modern cottages. In this section, one of the finest improvements is seen at Gramercy Place, an extension of Arctic avenue. Here the centre of the roadway is occupied by raised intervals of grass, along which, as well as upon the curbs, are ranged pedestals of Pompeian brick, similar to those guarding the entrance to St. Charles Place, and surmounted by handsome lanterns.

The greater hotels are nearly all between Pacific avenue and the ocean front, most of them in touch with the Boardwalk. Proceeding south and west from the Inlet along the Boardwalk, these, and the other principal features of the fashionable side of town, come into view in the following order:

Rhode Island Avenue: The Senate.
Massachusetts Avenue: The Lelande. The Iron Pier.
The Japanese Tea Garden occupies most of the next block.
New Jersey Avenue: The Rudolf.
St. Charles Place: The St. Charles.

States Avenue, a very broad highway, is bordered almost entirely by cottages.

Maryland Avenue: The Imperial, Hotel Portland and the Scarborough. Several extensive bathing-houses front on the Boardwalk.

Virginia Avenue: The Islesworth, Ponce de Leon, Majestic, Berkshire Inn, Brookehurst, Grand Atlantic, Irvington, Wiltshire, Ardmore, Monterey, Linden Hall, Clarendon and Albemarle.

At the foot of this avenue, opposite the Jackson Bath House, is the new Atlantic City Steel Pier.

Pennsylvania Avenue: The Seaside, Hotel Hoffman and the Lehman.

North Carolina Avenue: Haddon Hall and Chalfonte.

South Carolina Avenue: Somers Casino, Hotel Warwick, Tudor Hall, Manhattan, Stanley and Mentone.

Ocean Avenue: The Toboggan Slide, The Crystal Maze. This is a cottage avenue.

Tennessee Avenue: The west side is occupied by a range of twenty hotels, the Rossmore, near Pacific Avenue, being the largest.

In the succeeding block, which was the scene of the great fire of

last season, preparations are being made to build a number of costly hotels and other structures.

In front of this block is Young's Pier, extending 2000 feet into the surf. This has been largely rebuilt and greatly improved this season.

New York Avenue: Academy of Music, The Bryn Mawr Hotel,

Metropole, Hotel Koopman, The Maryland, Berkshire Inn, Chester Inn and several other medium hotels.

Kentucky Avenue: The Stratford, Berkely, Evard, Kenilworth, Hotel de Ville, Wellington, Runnymede, Boscobel, Westminster, Willard,

ALONG THE
SEA FRONT,
LOOKING EAST

Luray, Norwood, Wetherill, Hotel Richmond and other lesser establishments.

Bew's Hotel is one of the few fronting immediately upon the Boardwalk.

Illinois Avenue: The Windsor and the Traymore occupy opposite sides of this street. Just beyond is the handsome Casino building with its elaborate baths, parlors, ballroom and gardens.

Indiana Avenue: The Hotel Brighton, and opposite is the large costly cottage of Mr. Fred. Hemsley, owner of the Brighton and the Casino. Between this cottage and the sea is handsome Brighton Park.

Park Place: The grounds and building of the Convent of the Sacred Heart face Brighton Park, and beyond, toward Pacific Avenue, are the Chatham, the Revere and some other houses. The Mercer Memorial House being at the corner of Pacific Avenue.

Ohio Avenue: A large space is occupied by the buildings of the admirable Seashore House for Invalid Children. (See chapter devoted to this charity.)

Michigan Avenue: Hotel Dennis, The Shelbourne, Pennhurst, Arlington and Edison.

Arkansas Avenue: The Fortescue, and many other moderate-sized hotels, crowd this avenue, and along this section the Boardwalk is lined with restaurants, bath and amusement pavilions, etc., the same being true of Missouri Avenue.

The Boardwalk extends in its full width several blocks further, merging at Texas Avenue, into the remaining portion of the old walk. This marks the limits of the closely built portion of the city, which, however, is rapidly spreading toward pleasant and modern Chelsea just beyond.

It is expected that the permanent Boardwalk will soon be extended west from Texas Avenue through Chelsea, as this progressive suburb has appropriated the money to replace the old wooden walk which at present exists upon its sea front.

AT LOW TIDE

It has been well said that the Boardwalk and its miles of clustered structures, form but the frame for the real picture seen in the vast cosmopolitan. The true interest is in the cosmopolitans who are there to serve and to be served. The surging throngs that pass and repass, hour after hour, upon a summer's day find abundant diversion in the orientals who border their pathway, displaying strange and beautiful wares filled with the rich colorings of eastern dyes, and fashioned with the fantastic designs of far-away lands; they are beguiled by the comic mountebank, and enthralled by the promise of a glimpse into the future by the shrewd devotees of astrology.

The life of the world is arrayed here in all its varied panoply to amuse and divert, but, after all, the greatest, most impressive, most interesting sight is the vast, well-dressed, well-mannered, happy-faced crowd of Americans, bent solely upon enjoyment, thousands and thousands of them, a marching army of men and women, with half a dozen policemen to keep them in order. In any other country it would take regiments of armed troops, and at such a sight reigning monarchs would tremble in their palaces. There are days in summer when the population of Atlantic City is reinforced by scores of excursion trains, until the avenues, the Boardwalk and the beach are black with masses of pleasure seekers who aggregate a hundred and fifty thousand. Such a scene as this, familiar enough in the metropolis of the sea, would carry confusion, turmoil, perhaps anarchy in its wake, in any other land. It is a most inspiring object-lesson to the student, of the characteristics of a free people.

The Summer Multitudes

That this modern phenomenon is possible, is due to the orderly instincts of the people who come here; to the railroads which provide such unequalled excursion facilities, and to the government of the city which, tolerating much, still enforces respect for the rights of all.

To the wonders of America, as known to travelers from other parts of the world, must soon be added the new subject, "A Sunday Crowd at Atlantic City in July."

A SUNDAY CROWD

Atlantic City.   **Chapter VIII.**

Atlantic avenue, which as surveyed extends some nine miles, was in the long-ago days of local history the principal hotel street from which more or less precarious board footways wandered across the sand dunes to the little coops of bathing houses that dotted the high water mark.

Atlantic Avenue

ATLANTIC AVENUE
LOOKING EAST

A local regulation requires that all new buildings through the heart of the city upon Atlantic avenue shall be fireproof, and many substantial public and business buildings are the result. Among the most striking buildings of a permanent character upon Atlantic avenue are those of the Union National, Second National and Atlantic City National Banks. The Real Estate and Law Building is one of the largest in the city. The "Elks" Building at Maryland avenue and the Neptune Hose House are handsome structures.

A Great Business Thoroughfare

Banks are the most positive evidence of general prosperity. The institutions mentioned above should have more than passing notice.

The Union National Bank was organized August 14th, 1890, with Mr. Allen B. Endicott, President; Mr. E. P. Williams, Vice-President and Mr. J. G. Hammer, Cashier.

UNION NATIONAL BANK.

The Bank opened for business October 11th, 1890, at their temporary office, No. 1726 Atlantic avenue. On the 23d of February, 1892, the Bank moved to its present building at the corner of Atlantic and Kentucky aves. Mr. J. M. Aikman was elected Cashier, April 14th, 1892, and in 1894 Mr. Smith Conover was appointed Vice-President, on resignation of Doctor Williams. The present Board of Directors consists of A. B. Endicott, Smith Conover, C. J. Adams, F. A. Souder, Thompson Irvin, F. J. Dickerson, A. H. Bailey, J. H. Lippincott, Lewis P. Scott, J. D. Southwick and George H. Jackson. A. B. Endicott, President; Smith Conover, Vice-President, and J. M. Aikman, Cashier.

Their deposits aggregate $400,000, and surplus and undivided profits, $45,000.

From their central location and their courteous and liberal treatment of depositors their prospects for a large and rapid increase of business are very bright.

The Second National Bank has won a reputation as one of the foremost financial institutions of Atlantic City, being noted for its fairness and ample accommodations to the public. Its building is one of the most artistic and striking objects upon this busy avenue.

The capital of the bank is $100,000; undivided profit, $75,000; average deposits, $750,000. President, George F. Currie; Cashier, L. A. Down.

Ample banking accommodations like those afforded by such institutions as the Second National Bank, have far more than local significance, as they often determine the visit and length of stay of families of wealth, resident in the large cities, whose heads must keep in touch with the financial world. No single influence has contributed more to the growth of Atlantic City than its group of banks.

SECOND
NATIONAL BANK
ATLANTIC AVE

Among the business houses of Atlantic City, the important branch concern of the Bergner & Engel Brewing Co., of Philadelphia, occupies an important place. The long established popularity of the Bergner & Engel beers at the shore has been greatly increased by the facilities offered to the Atlantic City dealers, who have been uniformly loyal and appreciative of the progressive spirit shown in erecting the handsome building devoted by the company to its large business at this point.

The relative importance of good beer in satisfying the multitudes who resort to this great pleasure city, and in affording at all times a reliable and healthful summer beverage cannot be over-estimated. There is something especially felicitous in the union of a bottle of B. & E. and the cooling breezes of old ocean in their soothing effect upon tired and over-heated humanity, which has just poured down from the crowded and stifling city for a blessed smell of the salt air and a ramble along the Boardwalk.

Pacific avenue will probably always remain, as now, the leading cottage street. Many of the finest private homes in the city are ranged along its length. Most of the churches

Pacific Avenue

THE BERGNER & ENGEL
BREWING CO.'S BUILDING

are also upon this avenue, and at the corner of Illinois avenue is the costly Garden Hotel, seven floors in height. Among the churches are the First Presbyterian at Pennsylvania avenue, the First Baptist and St. James (Episcopal), North Carolina avenue, the Central Methodist and Friends' Meeting House at South Carolina avenue, German Presbyterian at Ocean avenue, St. Nicholas (Catholic) at Tennessee avenue, Church of the Ascension (Episcopal) at Kentucky avenue, St. Paul's (Methodist) at Ohio avenue, St. Andrew's (Lutheran) at Michigan avenue, and St. Monica (Catholic) at California avenue.

In the Suburbs The latest map of Atlantic City and its suburbs, as the growing settlements down the beach may be termed, is full of suggestion. The whole shore front, extending from the Inlet to Longport, has been plotted into avenues, those parallel with the sea being continuations of Atlantic, Pacific and the other principal avenues. About 130 blocks are located in these nine miles. In Chelsea, Chelsea Heights, Leonard, Ventnor, South Atlantic City, and in Longport, miles of grading have been done, and fine avenues now extend where not long since there existed nothing but a waste of sand hills, reminders of the site of Atlantic City in its original state. In all of these places many attractive hotels, private cottages and other permanent structures have been built. The electric railway binds the whole group by a rapid transit schedule in very comfortable cars, its termini being at the Inlet and at the steamboat wharf in Longport, where it connects with the ferry steamers for Ocean City and Somers' Point. The fare for the eight miles is ten cents. In summer the cars are open. The boats plying from Longport are large, handsome craft, regular pleasure yachts in fact, and form a part of a beautiful round trip, costing thirty cents, the return from Somers' Point being upon the dummy train via Pleasantville.   **A Pleasant Round Trip**

In considering the still unoccupied territory which will afford an opportunity to the Atlantic City of the future in which to grow, the beach upon Brigantine must be included. A great deal of work has been done here in the direction of development. The Brigantine Transit Company operates a ferry line from its pier near the Inlet and also a railroad along the beach to Little Egg Harbor Inlet seven miles away. The charge for the round trip is 25 cents. **Room to Spread**

But eleven per cent. of the total area of Absecon Island is yet built upon, a fact which may serve to impress such people who have concluded that the day for making money in Atlantic City real estate has gone by. There are still plenty of fortunes awaiting the future operator along the Jersey coast beside those buried there by Captain Kidd.

In the winter and spring of 1897, and for a year or so anterior to this time, a vast amount of work was found for the army of carpenters, masons and other mechanics in the building trades, in the very general enlargement of the principal hotels, following a great tidal wave of summer prosperity. In the spring of 1898 these same busy workers were employed upon a great number of high class private cottages. These are being built in all parts of the city and its outer borders. A wonderful transformation is being wrought in the neighborhood of the Inlet. Upon long neglected territory beautiful streets are now projected down to the surf upon one hand and far out upon the meadows to the thoroughfare and "basins" upon the other, and handsome cottages, in the best style of seashore architecture, are springing up from the ground as it by magic. The endless variety of these homes is bewildering, and the confidence shown by those who thus elect this as a summer residence is one of the surest indications of the greatness which still awaits the "City by the Sea."

The permanent population of Atlantic City in 1898 may probably be safely put as high as 25,000. In the summer season it may, at times, be multiplied by five or six. The systematic, orderly, tranquil way in which this remarkable place absorbs an army of visitors exceeding 200,000 persons, all eager, hungry and importunate—finds subsistence and beds for all of them and keeps them amused and happy between meals—is one of the wonders of the time. Any other resort would get "rattled" by such prodigious patronage. Nothing disturbs the mental poise of the citizen here, whether he owns a hotel, a store or a bazaar. He knows that the

people and their money will be along in due time and that "hard times" can't "down" the season to come.

In connection with Atlantic City the summer travel books issued by the railroad companies each season contain a list of about 400 hotels and boarding houses with location, terms of board, etc. Each of these, big and little, has its list of regular patrons, and thus, in a certain sense, the people upon the arrival of the long trains sort themselves out.

One of the most important lines of effort ever made by the authorities and hotel managers of Atlantic City has been its determined bid for convention business. There are held in the United States every year more than 1,000 regular conventions representing almost every possible human interest. The railroad companies all over the land from one ocean to the other are in constant correspondence in the interest of these gatherings, a large proportion of which are itinerant and thus, within a wide radius at least, open to the allurements of the seashore. The convention element is usually composed of intelligent and substantial people of the middle classes. They are well worth looking after as they are sure to go home and spread the fame of Atlantic City's greatness far and wide.

During the summer of 1897, the influential Trades' League of Philadelphia, an organization of above two thousand firms, having for its object the development of the city's trade, was instrumental, in co-operation with the Railroad Companies, in bringing to Philadelphia a series of eleven large excursions of merchants and their families, from various sections of the United States. In the programme prepared for their pleasure, a liberal portion of the time was wisely given to Atlantic City. The public officials and hotel proprietors gladly seconded the efforts of the Trades' League in making these excursionists "at home." It was decidedly the most effective advertisement this resort has ever gained.   **A Friendly Call**

As a pleasant sequel, on December 2nd, 1897, a committee of Atlantic City's officials, business and hotel men presented to the Trades' League, at its beautiful rooms in the Bourse, a highly artistic copy of resolutions duly adopted at a meeting held for the purpose, thanking the Trades' League for its valued recognition as an essential in a summer visit to the Quaker City. In reply to the address of presentation made by Mayor Sooy, Mr. Thomas Martindale, the Chairman of the Special Committee upon Merchants' Excursions, made the following remarks, which embody so much of prophesy and suggestion, that by request they were afterwards printed and illustrated. By permission of Mr. Martindale, the pamphlet is reproduced that its contents may be more effectually preserved.

Mr. Chairman and Gentlemen:

As you are all busy men—even now there is hardly one of you but is occasionally taking hold of his watch-chain and nervously thinking of the time—I will be brief. In the first place, Mr. Chairman and gentlemen, these Resolutions ought properly to be inscribed (in addition to the Trades' League) to the Passenger Railroads centering in our city, and also to the entire Press of Philadelphia, which accomplished so much in giving wide publicity to those excursions that have been the means of bringing us together in such a happy manner. I never knew the Philadelphia newspapers to be so united on any one topic; but on this theme of theirs, and ours, of last summer—that of trying to help Philadelphia and Atlantic City by bringing great multitudes to both cities—every single one of them rolled up its sleeves and spread the printers' ink for all it was worth. And the railroad officials were equally liberal in granting many excursions, which were run upon the most generous plan, both as to the quick movement of the trains, and their sumptuous accommodations.

I am a great believer in advertising, not only in advertising the individual business but in advertising a city as well. Where a business is "run down at the heel" the first thing a business man should do is to advertise. A community following one common purpose to elevate and improve the business of their city or town, can do it better by advertising their interests, as a city, than by any other method. Atlantic City shows a good example to all her sister cities, by being the foremost in advertising, and it is on that account, more perhaps than any other, that it has become the Brighton of Philadelphia, as Brighton is now the Atlantic City of London.

About Advertising

My first trip to Atlantic City was in 1875. On that occasion I reached the shore in three hours, but when I arrived there I was covered from head to foot with dust and dirt and cinders. It took me four hours to get back home. The result was, that I was so tired and worn out I had a horror of Atlantic City for a long time afterward, and I did not revisit the place for several years.

Bygone Discomforts

IN THE EARLY DAYS

As an idea of what the transportation facilities to Atlantic City may become in the next twenty-five years I would call your attention to the remarks of Mr. D. B. Martin, General Passenger Agent of the B. & O. R. R. in his speech made before the General Passenger Agents of the United States in St. Louis, October 19, 1897. Mr. Martin said: "The locomotive has reached its utmost development and will soon be overshadowed by the application of electricity. The inventive world is filled with the ghosts and shadows of inventions that are useful and accomplish the purpose of the inventors. The first stage of an improvement is the accomplishment of certain results; the second, and equally as important, whether these results can be attained at a cost which will justify their use. In the adoption, therefore, of electricity to the steam railroad, we are in the second stage of its development. The problem yet to be determined is, assuming that the railroad system now operated by steam can obtain the same results with electricity, will the increased cost result in increased traffic? Then, if the electric power should develop a speed greater than steam, the distance across the continent would be minimized, and the business man who takes his breakfast in New York could dine in St. Louis and sup in San Francisco, while the span of the continent would be as hours instead of days."

A Forecast

Thus, gentlemen, in twenty-five years from now, according to this General Passenger Agent's prediction it may be possible for a man to start from New York and land in San Francisco in one day. If this can be accomplished, or anything like it, why may we not expect that the distance between Philadelphia and Atlantic City can be covered in less than fifteen minutes, or say, in the same time it now takes us to go to our homes in West Philadelphia, from the centre of the city?

Fifteen minutes to the shore

In closing his address Mr. Martin said: "From horse-power through the city of Baltimore at the rate of one mile an hour to that of electricity at sixty miles an hour, in one generation, is such an advance that the possibilities of the future can hardly be conjectured, and the rapid progress that has been made in the application of this wonderful motor justifies the belief that the days of smoke, steam and fuel annoyances are numbered.

Within the last year a bicycle path between Philadelphia and your city has been built at considerable expense, which enables the cycler or the "cyclist crank" that turns the crank, to pedal his way down to Atlantic City in from two hours and forty-seven minutes (which I think is the record) to ten hours. I believe that this bicycle path will in the future be supplemented by a broad highway on which we can ride our wheels down with comfort in wet days as well as in the sunshine —a grand road, with a broad and smooth surface—a modern Appian Way, upon which the rich and pleasure-loving people, blessed with fine horses, can drive down from Philadelphia in their carriages, leaving here in the morning and reaching your luxurious hotels in the evening of the same day.

Cycling to the Sea

The first stage in the development of the United States as far as buildings are concerned was the era of the log house or cabin. And the next was that of the frame structure. Atlantic City has reached this latter stage and amplified it to its greatest limit, as your modern frame palaces fully demonstrate; but the next twenty-five years will show your buildings to be, as they must be, of iron and stone and of brick, as a measure of economy, as well as safety.

A Trans-Jersey Drive

A Port of Entry

I have a dream that within the next twenty-five years Atlantic City will be made a port of entry, as well as a harbor of refuge, which should have been an accomplished fact years and years ago.

Last season an innovation in the method of conducting business between our city, on the waters of the Delaware, and yours on the sands of the great ocean, was made by some of our leading houses of trade, in canvassing for orders in your city, and delivering the goods in their own wagons at your very doors. This innovation no doubt will broaden so that most of the large houses will conform to it in future seasons, and in addition thereto a number of houses will open branches of their business within your borders, equipping their stores in a manner befitting the character of their home concerns, and of your increased demands.

Your postal facilities will be largely bettered and increased. When I first went to Atlantic City you had but two mails a day and no free delivery. Now you have a free delivery four times a day, and I predict that it will be increased in the future to a delivery every sixty minutes. At the time I speak of we had no telephone. We now have it from Philadelphia to Atlantic City, but have to pay fifty cents every time we use it to telephone to you or for you to telephone to us, and the telephone company takes care that the charges are surely paid. The time will come when, as a subscriber, you can talk to us in Philadelphia or we to you in Atlantic City, without extra charge, just as we do now to Germantown, West Philadelphia or Camden.

To you hotel men I want to say a few words, not in the line of criticism, but as a stimulus to the great work of improvement and progress that is in store for you in the years to come. You have done well in the past; you must do equally well in the future. Here are some things that I think, and believe you will accomplish. I see, in the future, a grand museum erected in Atlantic City, not a catch-penny affair with a hand-organ playing at the door, with an admission fee of five, or ten, or twenty-five cents, but a noble museum in every sense of the word, projected and maintained upon a liberal scale and supported either by your Hotel Men's Association, or by your city, for the instruction and entertainment of the good people that come to you from out the world at large. I also see an aquarium established upon a generous plan. Why should you not have this aid to the education and amusement of the visitors that come from the different parts of our great country? You, that have the ocean filled with its living curiosities at your very feet—I say why shouldn't you have an aquarium for their display? You should have had this attraction, at least years ago. I also see in the same future, a magnificent Concert Hall, not a little

An Aquarium

hall with five or six musicians playing on stringed instruments, accompanied by a twanging harp, or an orchestrion grinding out a set of tunes each and all out of tune, but a massive hall with a large and efficient orchestra, which orchestra shall play for the benefit of the whole people. A Crystal Palace, too, will arise in Atlantic City, and become the talk of the nation. Your now famous Boardwalk will give way to a broad boulevard of stone

BOULEVARD,
CITY OF DOUGLAS,
ISLE OF MAN

and cement and iron. 'Twill be a boulevard wide enough and broad enough to accommodate lines of street cars, lines of carriages, lines of equestrian riders, lines of wheelmen, as well as the millions of pedestrians; and moreover, a boulevard massive enough to withstand the ravages of old Father Ocean, and battle successfully with his most furious and destructive moods.

A Port of the Manx
I have the pleasure of showing you here a picture of the City of Douglas in the Isle of Man. Just look at this grand boulevard built of iron and stone fronting and encircling this magnificent array of hotels and amusement places. It was built in 1875. At Douglas the ocean exerts ten times a greater power upon their stone walk than would be imposed on any board-walk or boulevard that you can build at Atlantic City, the currents, tides and storms being so much more severe over there than they are with you. Now I show you a picture of that same boulevard as assailed by the fiercest power of the ponderous waves which you see dashing over and above it. In spite of these severe storms, and of their

A STORM AT DOUGLAS, ISLE OF MAN

effects, this magnificent roadway and promenade is just as firm now as it was the day it was finished; and let me say that this same City of Douglas in the last century was credited with a population of only 810 people who lived by the precarious industry of the herring fishery; and that now it has a resident population of over 15,000, and that there is not a single frame structure in the whole city that I know of.

I also want to show you gentlemen this little picture of an ocean walk of stone and iron fronting the city of Scarborough, in the North of England. The scene shown here represents a storm severe enough to have washed a full rigged ship broadside up to, and upon this famed boulevard,

yet the storm that you now see here and hundreds of others that have since spent their fury on its firm foundation, have had little or no effect upon it, and it stands as firm to-day as it did half a century ago. **An English Resort**
In the City of Scarborough they not only have a grand museum, a great aquarium, and a " Spa," but they also have a very large and very fine

A STORM AT SCARBOROUGH, ENGLAND

Public Concert Hall, where on pleasant days the ladies bring their children, and with their knitting, their embroidery, or their favorite novel, remain for hours, while the gentlemen visit and chat, or flirt with them, and the children romp around or dance with childish abandon. Each and all are entranced by the grand music of the orchestra, which plays during the afternoon and evening the whole season long, and to the delight of visitors from all parts of the United Kingdom.

One of your up-to-date hotel men has sent out a circular to his patrons, the closing sentence of which is the following: "There is more to say in favor of Atlantic City, much more to say that charms and fascinates, of this City of the Sea, but do not take our word for it; come and see for yourselves." Now this too is my text; but if you bring the people here, give them more than you do give, and are giving them at the present time. I know that there are no better hotel accommodations to be found in the whole world than in Atlantic City, (provided you pay for them), whether that be at the rate of $3.00 a day or $4.00 a day, but give your patrons something besides your hotels to talk about; something to attract, something to instruct the young people of the United States, as well as their elders. Have them go home and tell about your wonderful Music Hall and your attractive Aquarium, your magnificent Crystal Palace with its bewildering glories of electric lighting, living waterfalls, and its things of beauty and things of pleasure. Let them also tell of their walks and the sights they have seen, and the people they have met, upon your grand boulevard of stone, of iron, and cement. All these things must not be catch-penny affairs, but big civic enterprises, big civic accomplishments, worthy of Atlantic City and in very truth of any city. Let them talk of Atlantic City as if it were another White City, as the exhibition buildings and grounds in Chicago were called during the World's Fair. Let them talk of the wonders of Atlantic City as people will talk of the wonders of Paris in the year 1900. Then you will have the visitors pour in upon you by the tens of thousands where they now come by the hundreds.

In conclusion, gentlemen, if you will help yourselves in the future, as you have helped yourselves in the past, and live up to the full measure of progress that the pressure of the times will demand of you for the next 25 years, the business men of Philadelphia must and will extend to you a helping hand, and the government of the United States must and will help you, not only to make Atlantic City a harbor of refuge, and a port of entry, but the greatest and most attractive seaside resort of the world."

Atlantic City.   Chapter VIII.

VACHT PIER

Upon a Summer Morn

The most picturesque feature of the Island at all times is found at the yacht wharf alongside of the great pavilion at the Inlet. It is worth while to bestir one's self at dawn upon a Summer morning and ride or walk briskly up to the Inlet, just to have a glimpse of the lively stir among the brigade of popular and enterprising "cap'ns" who are busy with the preparations for the expected rush of customers. *The Pleasure Fleet at the Inlet*

It takes a lot of marine housekeeping to run an Atlantic City sloop, or even a cat-boat. There's the regular morning swabbing down of the decks, the overhauling of cordage, looking after blocks, brass work, ballast, flag-halyards, reef-points, and all kinds of small but important nautical matters, not to mention the rugs and cushions which a capricious, exacting and effete civilization insists upon having. Very likely it's a dead calm and already insufferably hot out there upon the long wharf where the scores of craft poke their noses against the landing like so many mules at the crib, but the old salts don't mind it. They can tell you just to the minute and from what exact point of the compass the breeze will arrive; and so when the trolleys begin to bring the festive throngs from the hotels and cottages, dressed in every variation of nautical outfit, the whole scene takes on the look of a dress rehearsal of the "Pirates"; the "cracks" are already tacking to and fro in the jaws of the channel, and if you haven't a camera to catch the inspiring scene you are filled with vain regret. Then, some-

times, there are gray days when the rollers pour heavily over the bars, or sunlit days, full of fresh breezes from the seaward, when the big main-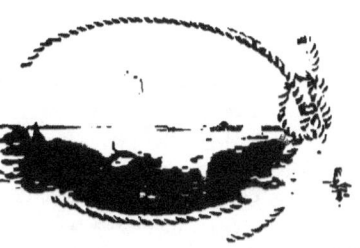
sails are double-reefed down upon the creaking booms, with little corners of jibs raised above the tip of the bowsprits, and the skippers speed to and fro in their oilskins through the splash and gleam of the dancing waters, just to show the crowds how safe and jolly it is out there. This is the opportunity for the youth who pines for glory from the sea, and for the pretty girl who "just loves a gale," and so they cling to the shrouds, with mackintoshes, skirts and ribbons all a-flutter, and for a little brief while are the observed of all observers as the sloop heels and plunges and races through the turmoil of waters. But, bless you! there's nothing to be alarmed at, for the sloop-man who brought his party into any sort of danger would presently have to hunt other occupation. If your "cap'n" says he will take you outside when things are looking ticklish from a landsman's point of view you can go right along just the same as if you were going to church, for it's fully as safe, and sometimes more exhilarating.

Just who or when the first Absecon boatman set up in the business of sailing pleasure parties is not a matter of verified history. The supply has followed the demand, and the demand came along with the very first excursionists who discovered Atlantic City. Thirty years ago the Inlet was a lively place, and twenty years since the prowess of the Inlet sailors and their boats was known to the whole coast.

There was the *Ocean Star*, Capt. J. A. Rider; the *Nautilus*, Capt. D. Chamberlain; the *C. L. Mott*, Capt. N. Sooy, and the *C. L. Harmer*, Capt. E. Endicott, all of the first-class. Then in the second-class were the *W. G. Bartlett*, Capt. Andy Snee; the *Neptune*, Capt. S. Gale; the *Ranger*, Capt. T. Conklin, who also ran the *Cecilda*. Among the smaller boats were the *G. W. Carpenter*, Capt. A. Holdzkom; *Orion*, Capt. H. Bowen; *Marshall*, Capt. G. Conover; *Regina Mary*, Capt. H. Snee; *Aunt Emily*, Capt. H. Smith; *J. H. Cousty*, Capt. Leeds Mills; *Katie*, Capt. D. Somers; *Viola*, Capt. J. Parker; *Champion*, Capt. J. M. Leeds, and the *Edwards*, Capt. Walter Somers.

Old Favorites

Over at Somers' Point in those days the Steelman boys had the *American Eagle*, the *Wave*, and the *Hinkley*, all well-known craft. Such things as "fin-keels" and "single-raters" and all that, were unheard of in those halcyon days, but those staunch old boats, full of the glory of red, white and blue paint, used to get over the salt water in a way that was inspiring and appetizing, and when there was a flutter of sea-gulls away out by the horizon, the race for the blue-fish was a beautiful thing to see.

The present fleet at the Inlet is large and still expanding. It includes the following craft and their captains:

Cat Yachts:— *Tom Gardner*, Con. Conover; *Carrie M.*, Walter Somers; *B. C. Pennington*, Norris Cramer; *Stella*, Henry Monroe; *Jennie J.*, Lem Conover; *Cameron*, Frank Gifford; *Star*, George Tomlinson; *Princess Bonnie*, Charles Gale; *Emma B.*, George Quinn; *Leira*, Isaac Conover; *Wm. Yewdall*, John Showell; *Ethel*, Ed Jones; *A. W. Beyer*, Charles Huntey; *Ralston*, Henry Endicott; *Laura*, A. Bowen; *William H.*, John Grahm; *Sallie*, A. Hickman; *Marcella*, Job Monroe; *Frances G.*, George

Gale; *Trilby,* Luke Conover; *Pert,* William Andrews; *Caddie B.,* Lewis Barrett; *Sparkle,* William Somers; *Nepaul,* H. H. Parker; *Katie,* William Lowder; *Harold,* Wash Watson; *Uncle Benny,* John Conover; *Anna,* Jas. Monroe; *Dart,* Sam Monroe; *Orville,* Captain Haunsley; *Carrie.* Dolph Parker; *Defender,* Abe Casto; *Albion,* Francis Parker; *Della,* Dan Showell; *Lettie,* Alfred Showell; *Prince Arthur,* Frank Doughty; *Blue Bird,* Fen Doughty; *L. S. Allen,* Frank Ducase; *Kenderton,* Ben Loveland; *C. S. Haines,* Ed Turner; *Mary,* Wm. Hammel; *Glide,* Ezra Somers; *Paterson,* Ben Bowen; *Lizzie,* Tom Bowen; *Katie Meher,* Sam Mills; *Belle,* Geo. W. Gale; *Kitty Clover,* John Dutch; *Majestic,* Andrew Monroe; *Pastime,* Ab Adams; *Snellenburg,* James Miller; *Lady Eldridge,* Charles Mathis; *Clara S.,* Mark Casto; *Sparta Fritz,* Gideon Conover; *Volunteer,* Nathan Parker; *Jennie,* H. Frambes; *Seabright,* Dan Giberson.

The Fleet of '98

Sloop Yachts :—*St. Charles,* E. A. Parker; *J. E. Maher,* Sam Gale; *Cornet,* Wm. Downs; *Volunteer,* Nic Sooy; *M. S. Quay,* Ben Sooy; *Alert,* Will Gale; *C. F. Whall,* Jim Downs; *Zella,* Lew Adams; *Morgan,* C. Foster; *Katie Becker,* P. Blackman; *Dreadnaught,* Joseph Higbee; *Tillie Covert,* James Mills; *Mascott,* Harry Parker; *Minerva,* D. Driscoll; *Parnell,* G. Mathis; *Carrie Egner,* James Parker.

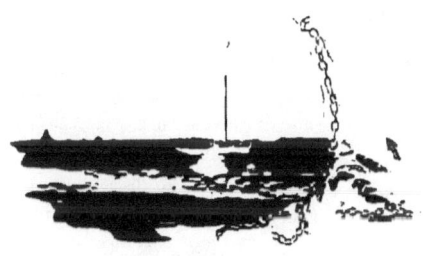

Atlantic City.   **Chapter IX.**

A Refuge from Illness and Care

"An idle sort of a place, where all day long
It seems like evening with the day's work done,
Where men haste not, because there is no haste,
And toil but little, for they've little need :
A restful corner, where the August breeze,
From softly listening finger on the lip,
At length from listlessness falls fast asleep,
Till there is no sound heard save, now and then,
The whet of scythe and heavy hoist of sail,
The dip of unseen oars, monotonous,
And softly breathing waves that doze below,
Too weak to more than turn themselves, complain,
And doze again."

Philadelphia is regarded as an especially healthful city, and justly so. No large city in the world boasts a death rate so low ; and yet Atlantic City, its near neighbor, and almost its suburb, has a record of 12.05 deaths per thousand in the year, or over eight deaths in the thousand better than Philadelphia, and almost exactly the same rate of mortality as Los Angeles, California, a city largely populated by Eastern invalids. It may be properly urged that among the permanent residents the percentage is still lower, as the rate given in the official statistics include the mortality among the vast number of persons who come here as invalids. It is not necessary to live throughout the year in Atlantic City in order to partake of the beneficence of its climate. It may be taken, like any other good tonic, for a season. If every over-taxed

A Health Record

business man, worn-out mother, or tired society woman would hie to Atlantic City when "that tired feeling" asserts itself and stay until it had quite given over the assault, regardless of the season of the year, the measure of their lives would be extended and their capacity for happiness vastly increased. Atlantic City is at the old stand, doing business all the year,

Winter Hospitality and there is never a time when the best hotels are caught napping. One can come here in the depths of winter and find every comfort obtainable in any large city in the country. It would be necessary to travel a long way southward to find an equal improvement in the temperature generally existing here as compared with New York and Philadelphia. There are exceptions to this rule. Palm trees and bananas do not thrive at Atlantic City, except in the sun-parlors and upon the dining-room tables. Sometimes the easterly storms smite the town, and for days it rains and snows and snows and rains, but just reflect how much worse things must be in the streets of Philadelphia, and how comfortably the hours go by in the bright sun-parlors with the latest magazines, cards, and the good company of scores of other sojourners just like yourself.

When a person of leisure is well ensconced in a good Atlantic City hotel in the winter the only thing that should tempt him or her to go away should be the pleasure of coming back.

Atlantic City. Chapter X.

Cottage life at Atlantic City is very like that which exists at other fashionable seashore communities. It implies a wide variety of diversions, from bathing to golf. It bestows upon the occupants a pleasant degree of privacy without loneliness. The cost of living, through the facilities with which all market supplies are to be had from both the Philadelphia markets and the fertile mainland, is rather less than "in town," while the brevity of the little journey upon express trains to and from Philadelphia makes it very practical for business men to "'tend to things" every day at their offices in the big city, and enjoy evenings, half-holidays and Sundays where cool breezes woo health, appetite and good sleep. Hundreds of busy men who have at first projected a cozy little place for the summer months have finally adopted Atlantic City as an all-the-year home, with a few midwinter weeks, perhaps, with friends in Philadelphia (to be repaid in the next Summer). They thus find a happy solution of the problems of economy, health and happiness.

In Private Cottages

A MODERN COTTAGE

Ideal Existence

Instances are plentiful where cottage owners have more than cleared their entire outlay through the advanced value of the land, and since it is the boast of the Atlantic City people that no property has ever been sold at a loss in the town, it is fair to presume that for many years yet to come a tasteful cottage well situated will prove a safe investment for its owner.

Palatial homes There are scores of beautiful residences here furnished upon a scale of splendor almost undreamed of by those who pass. Rich drapings, carvings and curios from every land are hidden away in the private apartments of these lovely homes; but it does not follow that these are prime essentials to the full enjoyment of shore life, or life anywhere else, for that matter. The family which now lives in the pent-up, solid brick, wooden-shuttered streets of the crowded Quaker City, or in any of its neighboring cities, can generally afford to have a cottage at Atlantic City and treat themselves, at last, to the glorious roominess of the "great out-doors" around them. Atlantic City seems to the casual observer to offer an abundant variety of occupations not yet over-filled. Twenty-five thousand people seem to have found it possible to live, work and enjoy life here successfully. To own a cottage at Atlantic City is to have a new insight into the brighter possibilities of life.

A COTTAGE ROW AT THE EAST END

Atlantic City.   Chapter VII.

Herbert James Tweedie, a high authority in the world of Golf, has authorized the statement in the chief periodical devoted to that fascinating diversion, that he had found near Atlantic City the "finest natural sand-bunkers in America." This means a whole volume of delightful promise to the devotee of the sport, although to the indifferent layman it may seem of but transient purport, but then what can you expect of the man who is indifferent about golf, and can't tell you the difference between a putting-green and a turnip-patch.

The Country Club

Mr. Tweedie was commissioned by the Country Club to put this favored place into orthodox shape for the game. The Country Club had bought one hundred and ten acres over upon the mainland, upon the seaward side of the Old Shore Road, and upon this property the links and the new club-house have been opened.

THE COUNTRY CLUB

The following adequate description of this social and athletic enterprise is taken from "Golf":

"The plans for the club-house show a commodious structure of a style of architecture most suitable to the surroundings and well adapted for the purpose for which it is intended. The building will be two stories high,

125 feet long and 30 feet wide, with porches on three sides that will form a promenade 12 feet wide and 200 feet in length.

Entering the main doorway the visitor will find himself in the public hall or exchange, a fine large apartment that will prove a pleasant meeting and lounging place for the members of the club and their friends. A large fireplace at one end of the exchange is fitted with an old-time crane and kettle, that will lend a rural air to the scene. Beyond the hall, at the end of the house, is located a handsome reception-room.

A Social Centre

On the opposite side of the entrance to the right will be the stairway leading to the second story; and beyond that will be the café. This room will be elegantly fitted up and supplied with all that such an establishment should have. Adjoining it will be the kitchen and pantry, rooms that will be complete in themselves and furnished with all the appliances necessary for the successful practice of the culinary art. Next to the kitchen will be the men's dressing-room, where will be found plenty of lockers, shower baths and other conveniences.

The second floor will be devoted principally to the use of the ladies. A dressing-room for their use, with baths connected, will be located over the café. The hall over the exchange will resemble a balcony, similar to that at the Ocean County Hunt and Country Club, of Lakewood. Opening off this balcony on one side will be a small sitting-room or den. On the other side of the house, overlooking the golf course, is a porch that will be enclosed with glass, after the manner of a sun-parlor. In the end of the house, over the reception-room, will be the billiard-room, and at the other end there will be three large and airy bedchambers.

Many Comforts

The house is located in a commanding position facing the bay, and a circular drive will wind through the grounds from the main entrance to the club. An old farm-house has been moved from its original site and rebuilt near the main entrance. It will be used as a place of residence for the greenkeeper.

The Stables　　There will be ample stable-room on the premises. The stable will now accommodate twenty-two horses, and this capacity will be increased. Sheds are being built large enough to accommodate vehicles of all kinds, including the tally-ho coaches that will make frequent trips to the grounds.

A long-distance telephone service will be a convenience, and every modern contrivance has been arranged for the comfort of the members and guests. The putting greens are thoroughly worthy of the name, being fully sixty feet square and carefully laid down with turf brought all the way from Pennsylvania. From many points the course with its surroundings closely resembles the famous Luffness Links, on the Firth of Forth.　　**The Pines**

The pine woods, which make a delightful background on the land side, protect the links from the north winds in winter, and will enable the club to keep the grounds open the entire year.

The famous bicycle path leading from Philadelphia to Atlantic City passes right along beside the course and will no doubt be a very popular mode of access to the club.

Adjoining the golf links is the polo field, while the tennis courts, football, cricket and baseball grounds and shooting traps are all conveniently located.

The officers of the club have generously promoted this enterprise for the good of the cottage and permanent residents of Atlantic City, who were hitherto unprovided with suitable accommodation for field sports. All visitors, however, profit by the accession of this real seaside golf links, as it will only be necessary for them to mention GOLF at the desks of either of the hotels before mentioned to freely tread the springy turf here consecrated to the Royal and Ancient Game.

The present list of officers is as follows: Fredk. Hemsley, president; J. Haines Lippincott, vice-president; Chas. Evans, treasurer; Joseph H. Borton, chairman; James B. Reilly, A. Ogden Dayton, Richard F. Loper, Joseph Thompson, E. S. Lee, directors; James D. Southwick, secretary.

Among the many diversions of this fascinating place, a month's stay may include golfing, cycling, polo, tennis, cricket, football, baseball, billiards, quoits, shuffleboard, euchre parties, dancing, shooting (snipe, marlin, black duck, mallard, teal), fishing (bluefish, sheepshead, drum, cod, herring, mackerel, seabass and weakfish), crabbing, yachting, rowing, promenading, surf-bathing, etc.   *Varied Sports*

In short, at Atlantic City one can obtain more genuine pleasure to the square inch than in any other spot the writer is familiar with."

Atlantic City. Chapter XIII.

A couple of weeks in Lent at Atlantic City after the winter's exhausting gaieties has been voted the proper thing by the inner circles of fashion, and the early spring influx is counted upon in these recent years with great certainty. It is decidedly an exclusive patronage and demands the best of everything. At this time one encounters the people of wealth and leisure from all over the country who propose, later, to fill the great trans-Atlantic steamships for the tour of Europe. National dignitaries from the capital, judges of courts, famous divines, officers of the army and navy, railway magnates, bank presidents, eminent politicians and their families, gossip, jostle, and throw dignity to the winds upon the great Boardwalk. Affairs of vast import are discussed and settled upon the porches of the big hotels; there is a great coming and going of extra parlor cars, and then the Lenten pilgrims take their flight full of the consciousness of time well spent, if not of sins properly expiated. The landlords bank the proceeds of this Providential fashion, and calmly wait for the multitude which will pour in along with the first hot wave of the summer.

The Lenten Season

LENTEN PENITENTS

The Awakening

Lent is, too, the popular awakening from the relative torpidity of the winter. The cosmopolitans who throng in the bazars along the Boardwalk begin to come back from the south with their oriental goods and catching trifles; the house-owners utilize their early spring outing to "fix up" their properties; hotels, big and little, are being painted; yachts are overhauled and got ready for the season at the Inlet, and so it goes. Nowhere else does Easter reign as a special season of holiday. Here, as in many other things, Atlantic City is original.

The Lenten period may be regarded as the most joyous time in the cycle of the year, for it is rich with the forecast of prosperity and pleasure. About this time the society columns of the daily papers in the leading cities, which have in the drear winter time made but brief and grudging mention of the existence of Atlantic City, begin to blossom with long lists of social leaders and followers who are now registered at the various fashionable hotels, while the more important enlargements of hotels and other betterments in the community are detailed in flowery language. Promptly upon the heels of these disinterested items comes the advertising man, who knows better than anyone else when the harvest is ripe for the scythe.

THE ROAD TO THE SEA

The Joyous Sea   Even the surf along the beach seems to roar joyously in Lent, and the ripples that play upon the bosom of the Thoroughfare and along the wide reaches of the bays have a gladsome gurgle. The gunner and the ducks are heard and seen in the sedges. The husbandman and the golfer are both hard at work upon the slope of the mainland; briefly, all nature is happy.

Lent, in other places, may stand for metaphorical sackcloth and ashes. Here, by the sea, it expresses quite a different sentiment.

The famous cycle road across New Jersey now teems with life awheel. Upon pleasant Sundays, when the wind is westward, the wheelmen and wheelwomen come in shoals.

One of the great events of the past year, relating to the progress of Atlantic City's interests, was the completion of the now famous cycling

Cycle Road to Atlantic City

road across New Jersey. The initial portion of this very popular route out of Camden and Gloucester is over the excellent White Horse Pike, via Berlin and Blue Anchor. From the latter point the course is almost an air line parallel with the railroad lines through Winslow Junction, Rosedale, Hammonton, Da Costa, Elmwood, Egg Harbor and Absecon, turning to the right at the latter place to Pleasantville, and thence across the meadows. At numerous points along the road "Cyclers' Rests" and hotels built with special reference to the patronage of the wheeling element have come into existence, and upon Sundays, especially, the cyclers in clubs, groups, pairs, and singly have been simply uncountable as they sped to and fro upon this level course. They have added a large and joyous contingent to the population by the sea, not only in the crowded season, but both in spring and autumn. From Pleasantville cycling tourists can go down the coast to Cape May, or via Barnegat to the fine cycling district around Long Branch, with but brief stretches of poor road. It seems superfluous to call attention to the many miles of perfect riding within the limits of Atlantic City and down the Island to Longport, not to mention the beautiful stretch of hard beach at low tide. The cycling regulations are similar to those of other cities, and the wheelman who observes the ordinary rules by which he is guided elsewhere will have no cause to complain of the liberality of the city toward this important class of visitors.

Atlantic City.   Chapter XIIII.

The annual report of the City Controller, Mr. A. M. Heston, indicates in detail the various items of public property which aggregated September 6, 1897, in value $1,591,646.14, including $138,929.85 expended upon the Boardwalk. The indebtedness of the Corporation amounted at that date to $7,175,433.31; this included water bonds slightly in excess of $300,000.

Some City Matters

The per capita debt of Atlantic City as compared with many other cities of the state, notably, Newark, Jersey City, Elizabeth, Orange, New Brunswick, Bayonne, Rahway and Asbury Park is highly favorable.

The item of Police cost $28,174.79; and the maintenance of Fire Department, $16,608.00.

Values and Finances from Report of 1898

The assessable property is rated for taxation at $13,357,523, the actual value being generally held to be about three times that amount at the present time.

Among the firemen of the United States the Atlantic City fire service has a great reputation. Although composed of but seven companies all told it has often demonstrated its remarkable ability to conquer the frequent fires which are inevitable in a city built so largely of wood. The chief, engineers, drivers and tillermen are upon the city pay roll. The rank and file of the companies are volunteers. The oldest company is the United States, No. 1. This company has two engines of the Silsby type and also a chemical engine. The other companies are Atlantic No. 2, a Clapp and Jones engine; Neptune Hose, No. 1, a La France engine; Good Will Hook and Ladder, No. 1, a Holloway chemical engine and a Hayes truck; Beach

Pirates Chemical, No. 1, one Holloway chemical engine; Chelsea, No. 6, a chemical engine and combination truck; Rescue Hook and Ladder, No. 2, a Gleason & Bailey truck.

The Fire Fighters

The hose carriages at the several fire-houses are provided with about two and a half miles of hose.

The cost of the department in 1897 was $31,540.73. The Gamewell Fire Alarm System is in use.

Both gas and electricity are employed as public illuminants, and the use of incandescent electric lighting is very general in the larger hotels.

In the matter of good wholesome water, Atlantic City is far ahead of Philadelphia; many unfailing artesian wells, some of which pierce the earth to the depth of a thousand feet, supply the big hotels and reinforce the public supply which comes seven miles across the marsh in pipes from the mainland, where the pumping station and stand-pipes are located. Nearly fifty miles of pipe are laid in the city, with which are connected about 450 fire-plugs. The total cost of the waterworks has been $877,957.92.

Light and Water

Realizing the great importance of safeguarding the city from the effects of inefficient disposal of sewerage, the most costly and scientific methods have been adopted, with the result that this problem, so difficult of solution, especially in a town built upon a perfect level, has been mastered. Upon the borders of the meadows a large receiving pit, walled and cemented, is used as a central receiver; this is ventilated by a lofty tower; the inflow is forced onward by steam-power to a series of filter beds so far removed from the city as to preclude any possible danger, even in midsummer. No sewerage whatever is allowed to contaminate the salt water thoroughfares or the open sea in front. All garbage is burned at a crematory.

Sewerage

Military Company F, Sixth Regiment, N. J., National Guard has its headquarters at Atlantic City.

The Morris Guards, an independent company, is also one of the city's attractions upon occasion of parades. The armory of this company is a favorite place for entertainments.

In the summer of 1898 when the Atlantic Coast seemed to be in danger from the Spanish fleet under Admiral Cervera, the fever of military spirit spread everywhere among the young men of Atlantic City. Active measures were taken for defence against landing parties of the enemy, and in such a contingency the local troops would have certainly given a good account of themselves. For a time the generality of the resident and large property owners were considerably excited, especially in view of the news from the eastern resorts where the Yankees were moving everything portable far inland. It was difficult to rent cottages, and matters looked black for the hotels. Nevertheless the people recovered their mental balance, the crowds came as usual and the season was a great success. Many of the soldiers gallantly marched away with the splendid New Jersey regiments and took an active part in the campaign as volunteers of Uncle Sam.

At the Nation's Call

Atlantic City. Chapter XIV.

One of the early institutions of the young city was the beneficent though modest charity known as the Children's Seashore House, founded just a quarter of a century ago, and intended for the recuperation of babies and small children, generally in charge of the mothers. This idea originated in Philadelphia where as a matter of course the majority of its beneficiaries live. It would be impossible to measure, even approximately, by any known formula, the great good accomplished at this juvenile invalids' retreat. The incorporators were James S. Whitney, J. Shipley Newlin, W. L. Rehn, René Guillou, Samuel Middleton, Francis W. Lewis, M. D., Mrs. Elizabeth F. Whitney, Mrs. Cynthia Guillou, Mrs. Annie E. Middleton and Miss Catharine C. Biddle.

Children's Seashore House

A Splendid Charity

In July, 1883, the institution took possession of a new and commodious building at the foot of Ohio avenue. Since that time it has been further extended by the addition of no less than fourteen lesser buildings, the gifts of guests in the several hotels for which they are respectively named. These cottages consist of one dormitory room each, neatly furnished. The capacity of the establishment is now sufficient to entertain one hundred children and thirty mothers. The selection of those who are to receive the benefits of a seashore rest at this noble charity is uninfluenced by any considerations of creed, race, or color. Children over three years of age are cared for in the wards of the main building by attentive

nurses. The little ones with their mothers are assigned to the cottages. Each mother in care of a sick child may have no other child with her. Serious cases requiring close attention and quiet are secluded in a special building immediately on the beach.

The institution has a resident physician, staff of nurses and matron. A proportion of the inmates are received without charge, the number being based upon the current revenues at command. Those who can afford it, pay board at the rate of $3.00 per week, which includes medical attendance and washing. Railroad tickets are also furnished at a reduced rate.

Visitors are welcome every afternoon between three and five o'clock, and upon Tuesday and Friday mornings from half past nine to half past ten o'clock.

To the person of kindly impulses the sight of scores of these little ones with their wan and tired mothers, gradually winning for themselves some little share of God's sunshine and the blessings of new strength as they romp or recline upon the sands, is to gain for the Children's Seashore House new and very welcome friends and supporters.

A wide-spread impression is current that the world, and more particularly Atlantic City, exists principally for the benefit and pleasure of the young. This in its application at large is an old idea which has been popular from the most remote bounds of history.

If our peerless city of the sands attracts the gay and youthful by its perennial round of varied pleasure; if it is a joy to the tired mother and fagged father to watch their little tots industriously toiling with spades and buckets in the clean, wholesome, gray sand, it is a glowing satisfaction to the impartial observer to note the wonderfully large proportion of aged

For Young and Old

people in the rolling-chairs and in all the bright comfortable nooks along the Boardwalk; to see with what loving care they are attended, and how grateful the fresh stimulating sea-breeze is to their senses. To the old more than any others of our American people who throng here, Atlantic City is a blessing, and an opportunity in prolonging and brightening the later years of life. Here the still heaving waves of past reverses which have surged over them; the deep sorrows which have torn their hearts are drowned in the brightness of the present, and lost in the tumult of the restless sea which goes on forever beating the sands with its stately, graceful billows, whose deep voice lulls us to rest in the daytime and follows us in our dreams at night.

This is the true story of one aged *habitue* of the Boardwalk who may be seen every day, strong, erect and keen-eyed among the throng of pedestrians:

The Story of an Old Man

"Fourteen years ago, I had arrived at the age of sixty years. All of my life, from the close of my college days, I had worked steadily and with success to the end that my wife and children should escape the bitterness of that poverty of which I had been a witness in my father's home. At sixty I was a worn-out man, but I was worth nearly half a million dollars. I believed it to be safely invested, but a little group of men, none of whom I had ever met, sat together in a room in Wall street, New York, and willed otherwise. Through those modern weapons of the legalized robber, combination and reorganization, my fortune was nearly swept away. It was weeks before I realized the full extent of my loss. My first impulse was to return to the business world and try to rebuild my property, but in the short five years of my absence nearly all of the men I had known and trusted had been replaced by other and younger workers. I was a physical and a mental wreck. Out of the remnants of our means, my wife and sons paid the cost of a year in Europe. We wandered from land to land, but the ghost of my misfortune threw its gaunt shadow across my pathway wherever we went. Once more we were in America. An old friend who had been content with smaller prizes in life than those most of us reach for, invited us to visit his little farm out in Jersey.

Return to Simplicity

At first I was almost disgusted at the primitive style of life I found under my friend's roof. Most of the modern indispensables with which we were in daily contact in the city, were conspicuous by their absence. But there was an abundance of good substantial food. I began to sleep—to sleep as I hadn't slept since I was a little boy, tired out after a holiday afternoon. The light of content began to drive the old tenant, worry, from the eyes of my dear wife. In the stillness of the evenings as we sat and smoked happily upon the porch, I gathered in some of my old comrade's philosophy, and began to feel ashamed when I thought of the two occasions in years gone by when I had prepared to destroy myself. Well, in the end,

In Business by the Sea

we bought a little place of a few acres near our host, and within an hour's ride of either the city or the shore. One of our daughters and her husband came to live with us. Four years ago my two sons rented a cottage here at Atlantic City and brought us down to share it. We have now built our home here. My sons have developed a good business "upon the avenue." My son-in-law, God bless him! runs the farm, and runs it well. I spend my time about equally between the little farm and this magnificent sanitarium, the Boardwalk. I look back upon the years that have gone as one remembers some dreadful nightmare. Here we have found, my wife and I, the happiest part of our lives. You must come to dinner with me and meet her. We have just an hour to spare, let's walk to the Inlet and back."

Atlantic City.   Chapter IV.

Nowhere outside of a minstrel show is there a place which offers more temptation to good honest laughter than the Boardwalk. It's worth while to make the little journey hither just for the health-giving benefits of wholesome mirth. Something quaint or funny is always happening. There are so many odd-looking people mixed up with the great crowds, such bizarre bathing costumes, such pranks, such fun; and if one has a keen ear, so many humorous suggests (quite without the need of eavesdropping,) float in upon the understanding and tickle the fancy.

Along the Boardwalk

One recent morning an elderly lady, evidently upon her first visit, and much impressed by the healthful advantages of Atlantic City, found opportunity to confide in one of the big, handsome men of the life-saving service, a robust native of the sands. "How I do wish" said she, "my boy John was here now; he ain't ever seen the ocean, and it would do him a world of good, don't you think so?"

A Healthy Spot

"Yes marm," agreed the guard; "there isn't a better place to get well and have a big appetite in, anywhere in the world."

"Well, I guess that's so; you look like it; guess you was never sick in your life nor weak either; I guess you didn't come here for your health?" continued the visitor.

104

"Madame," said the guard, solemnly, "you may not believe it, but when I arrived here I was perhaps as weak as any human being you ever saw; I had no use of my limbs; I couldn't walk nor feed myself; I did not realize where I was."

"Goodness gracious!" she exclaimed with astonishment; "how did you ever live through it?"

"I had to, marm, although I was toothless, could not speak a word, and was dependent upon those around me for everything I needed. But as soon as I got here I began to pick up. The climate agreed with me. My legs and arms began to get strong, my voice developed, and I gained in weight every week. I have never been sick a day since that time."

"How interesting!" said the visitor. "How many years ago did you come here?"

"Thirty-one years, marm."

"Why, you must have been a baby!"

"Of course I was, marm. I was born here."

The Unprofitable Sign

Far down the Boardwalk, toward Texas avenue, a fat lobster-hued German has a "bathing plant." His rotund form was observed as the centre of a highly interested crowd in which the "party of the second part" was a lathy individual with stringy locks damp with recent sea-water.

"Holt on von minud," shouted the proprietor. "You can no leaf dese blace out so you not bay me for dot bat!"

"'Pay you for that bath'?" exclaimed the lathy one, in tones of astonishment. "Who said anything about paying?"

"I say somedings about dot."

"You do?"

"Yaw, I say you moost bay me for dot bat!"

"You say that the kind of bath I had don't cost anything," argued the wet-haired man.

"I no say any sooch tam foolishness!"

"What's that reading on your sign then?"

"Hot sign reats, Durkish bats, vapor bats unt sponge bats," repeated the German.

"Well, ain't that plain enough. I didn't have any money, so I took a sponge bath—see?"

The German eyed his sign with slowly gathering disgust, and an hour later a sign artist was busy obliterating the announcement of this unprofitable branch of the business.

On Rollers   The rolling-chair is a most essential factor in the life of the Boardwalk. We are moved, when we consider the matter, with sincere pity for our ancestors who had neither porches, hammocks, or rolling-chairs, who had, indeed, no Atlantic City. The rolling-chair made its debut as an ambulatory convenience at the great Centennial Exhibition twenty-two years ago. It filled the highways and by-ways of the Columbian Exposition at Chicago, but in its present perfection of comfort and grace it is only to be found upon the Boardwalk of Atlantic City. Upon the bright Sundays of springtime cohorts of rolling-chairs are constantly advancing, passing and receding into the throng. Reserve brigades of rolling chairs are ranged in line of battle at frequent intervals, and the rivalry of the rolling-chair magnates sometimes stirs Atlantic City to the profoundest depths of excitement. Some rolling-chairs are "built for two," but as a general thing the "conductor" carries only a single fare. The prettiest of these vehicles is built of basket work which glows richly under its varnish and which has a swan's neck prow rising well in front. In the winter and spring the passenger is buried in warm fur-robes, in summer bright blankets of light texture give a touch of barbaric color to the ordinarily sombre-hued American crowd. Flat Japanese umbrellas are rigged above the rolling-chairs, and when you have seen a pretty girl thus entramed, her lovely eyes drowsing in calm content, you have looked upon the finest picture you ever saw, and ought to be thankful that the Boardwalk, its rolling-chairs and its bewitching maidens exist.

No truthful mention of the Boardwalk can be made which fails to recognize its swarm of gamins, white and black. Atlantic City's resident population is abnormally active and enterprising. There is so much to be done in properly taking care of and still further extending the modern Atlantis which they have built. It is said that there are business men so closely occupied up along Atlantic avenue that they have never been down to see the new Boardwalk. But if the adults of the male element are thrifty and hustling in their ways, their progressive tendencies are as the movement of a glacier when compared with that which impels the gamin of the beach. This joyous creature leads a highly exciting and varied existence. He is in evidence at every storm centre of accident or incident. His senses are acute through long attrition with an ever changing multitude, and his coin-beguiling inventions are numberless. His mornings and evenings are devoted very generally to the dissemination of news, and he serves it hot. The intermediate period is given to disinterested anxiety for your comfort. If you stop in your walk for a moment to think of a word he charges upon you by the dozen ready to think of it for you. It is the gamin who navigates the unwilling donkeys along the beach for the joy of infantile riders, and who troops enviously after the haughty "caddies" attendant upon the self-absorbed golfers who golf upon

The Gamins of the Beach

A LET BUSIN

the sand at low-tide, but if you want to see the gamin at his best just throw a handful of pennies into the dry sand below the Boardwalk. When a wreck comes in your beach gamin is a stormy petrel. One of these days, very likely he will get a place in the Life Saving Service. These hardy soldiers of humanity were all beach boys once. Every beach boy can swim like a duck or handle a boat with the best of the graybeards at the inlet pier. He can tell you the name and the skipper of every little dot of a craft in sight away out there among the blue-fish. His soul is filled with contempt for any duffer at the helm who misses stays on a tack. He is resourceful beyond his years. Not very long ago one of these youngsters captured a prize just off shore in the shape of a cask of wine from some unfortunate cast-away coaster. Bigger boats and bigger boys were after the same cask. It was too heavy to lift into the boat, so he managed to tow it into a shallow, jumped overboard, sank his boat under the cask, bailed out with his cap and then got his flotsam to his daddy's wharf in the inlet.

BOSS OF THE BEACH DONKEY

The beach gamin is the pet aversion of the small but dignified nurse girls, who love to sit under the shade of the pavilions upon a shawl and read "Lady Desmonde's Secret or the Mystery of the Haunted Manse" while their wayward charges stake out claims and prospect with picks and shovels close under the heels of the untamed and impetuous donkeys. But the gamin and the girl will look at each other with different eyes some of these days. They will set up a little home over upon the seaward side of Arctic avenue, and a new generation of beach boys will be selling papers, running races and getting into everybody's way in the same cheerful, impudent, delightful fashion that you may see on any sunny day along the miniature world of the Boardwalk.

If, in the glare and color of morning and the fashionable array of afternoon the Boardwalk is attractive, at night it becomes fascinating. When the full moon glows and rises close upon the fading of the day, its white radiance comes tremulously across the sleepy sea to our very feet, touching a thousand features of the scene, which, in daylight are crude and garish, with a brush dipped in silver and revealing the long array of hotels as a veritable "white city" all aglow with gleam from a thousand casements.

Evening Scenes

The great arc lamps along the promenade cast dense contrasts of light and purple shadow, all the colors of the prism pour out from the hundreds of shops and shows of all sorts. Every inclined pathway from the hotels leading up to this pedestrian boulevard adds its tributary stream of gay humanity to the concourse of promenaders which have already filled the walk, the pavilions, and every place of attraction to repletion. The strident voice of the ticket seller and the fakir is heard above the roar of the toboggan, and the melody of the elite orchestra is hopelessly confused in the less classical but ever popular music of the hurdy-gurdy.

Nearly twenty centuries ago Glaucus folded his toga lovingly about the beautiful form of Ione as they wandered under the witching light of this same old moon, upon the crescent strand of Pompeii, the Atlantic City of Patrician Rome, the blue waters of the Bay of Naples splashed at their feet, the far lights of the fleets of Egypt and the orient twinkled in the offing, the soft music of slaves touching the cithera floated out from festive villas, and the magic of the summer night held them in the sweet spell of its happy influence, and thus the "old, old story" is rehearsed in unconscious emulation of those classic lovers along the sands and in many a shadowy nook between the inlet and Chelsea upon every rapturous summer night that draws its velvet curtain over the great pleasure resort of modern America.

Love by the Sea Summer love has oft been spoken of, and where but at Atlantic City can it be found in its prime? Together from early morn to dewy eve, in

FLOWERS AND
SUNSHINE

the fishing expeditions, the bath, the ballroom, and the twilight promenade, that loving couple we see at every turn would appear to the unobserved visitor to be the most devoted pair of lovers the world has ever seen. Their shy retreats to cosy corners, their cunning escapes from the prying eyes of mamma or the inquisitive looks of papa stamp them as strategists, while their rapt looks and tender salutations stamp them as loved and loving. And what does it all amount to? Nothing, absolutely nothing. He leaves, and his departure is attended with a tender parting at the train. She returns to the hotel or the cottage, perhaps, to start a new flirtation or maybe to mourn over the old one. The summer draws to a close and she goes back to her home. He moves in one set and she in another of our Quaker City aristocracy, and the consequence is that were barriers of iron, were the wall of China itself to be raised up between them, their separation could not be more complete. Like oil and water, up-town and down-town society do not mingle when within the sacred precincts of the City of Brotherly Love. So, of course, all intercourse is at an end. A cold bow and stately nod take the place of the familiar salutation at the seaside, and the signs of love upon these young hearts are as surely effaced by Dame Grundy as the footsteps they made together on the sands of the Atlantic are effaced by Dame Nature and her satellites, the waves.

Atlantic City.   Chapter XVI.

An incident in the history of Atlantic City which deserves to be preserved is the memorable snow blockade of February 12th, 13th and 14th, 1899. The City by the Sea has been more than once cut off from the outer world by phenomenal tides and suffered with the rest of the country in the blizzard of 1888, but upon this occasion she was fairly "bottled up," and this is not to be wondered at when the same conditions existed in all sections of Philadelphia's suburbs.   *Off Days at the Shore*

A newspaper dispatch gave the following condensed report of the situation:

In the Drifts   "With the wind blowing at the rate of forty miles an hour, a hurricane promised by the Weather Bureau for to-morrow, and the snow still falling, efforts of man to break the drifts are worse than useless. Not a train has entered or left this city since yesterday afternoon. Officials of the Pennsylvania Railroad started two engines out this morning to open up the road, but they only got as far as Egg Harbor, twenty miles distant, when they came to a final standstill and at last reports were still stuck in the drifts. The Reading Railway to-morrow will put to work every man that can be hired and an attempt will be made to shovel the snow from the tracks, but it looks like an almost helpless task.

The snowfall has been actually three times as heavy as during the memorable blizzard of March, 1888, although the wind was much higher then. A total of twenty-one inches of snow has fallen up to this evening, but the size of the drifts would lead to the supposition that the fall had been much heavier. The milk supply is entirely cut off and there is a great demand for the condensed article, but there is no danger of any serious famine.

There are enough provisions in the city to last at least two weeks, and the coal supply will probably hold out equally as long.

Scores of visitors went to the beach front during the day, in spite of the storm, to witness the novel sight of a frozen ocean. The wind had broken up the ice in the bays and it drifted down along the beach, filling the ocean with huge cakes that had the appearance of a solid mass. The ice is piled up on the beach at high water mark in great walls. No damage to shipping has been reported here, but communication with other life-saving stations along the coast is shut off."

The Flow of Enjoyments

Despite this isolation the coast folks managed to have a good time. The round of gayety went merrily on. It was cold, it is true. When the official records of the Weather Bureau show that the mercury has been doing the cake-walk in the neighborhood of the zero point, it would be useless to claim that June-like balminess had prevailed. But there was a peculiar something about it all that made one long for the open air, be the glowing coals in the parlor grate ever so attractive.

Sunny Corners

This had the effect of bringing many strollers out on the Boardwalk every afternoon, in spite of the wintry winds ; and when people once got out o' doors they were not willing to return as long as the nipping breezes could be borne. There were many sunny nooks along the walk where it was possible to rest for a short time, and these coveted places were in great demand. Even the devotees of the rolling chair habit were able to indulge their fad in comparative comfort. Well muffled up in furs and blankets, they were pushed along as though it were spring time, albeit the frosty air put a little more than the usual vim into the movements of the pushers.

Rainy Day Philosophy

To-day it rains. The waters prevail upon the face of the earth. As this visitation of dampness is not peculiar to this point alone, the force of the above observation is in some degree weakened. But it is needful to speak of it, in explanation of the fact that the sojourners at our various hostelries are at the present moment, as with one accord, in a state of torpidity sad to behold. They sit about here and there, just out of reach of the eaves drippings, looking for all the world like a lot of chickens on a very wet day in a farm-yard. A few have aroused their sluggish blood sufficiently to go down by the beach, and, protected by some one of the roomy pavilions, gaze out pensively over the storm-chafed waste of waters. Many have gone to

INDOOR COMFORT

"the city." Mondays always bring about a greater exodus than other days, but to-day many of the departures were occasioned by the adverse weather. The summer visitor flies like a bright-plumed songster before the slightest approach of skies overcast.

To leave the seashore for no better reason than a day or so of unkind weather is unwise—partly because the blue skies, which succeed almost

The Stormy Sea

invariably, will look all the brighter for the contrast, and again because the sea, to one who loves the beautiful, presents new charms at such times not to be disregarded. To stand in a sheltered place and watch the surging, inrushing billows lashed to a white fury is charming, but to view the waters illumed by the fitful electric glare, leaping out of the blackness of night, the deep diapason of the thunder mingling with the surf's unceasing roar, is to add another page to one's memories of the sublime.

The occupants of three hotels join in a revel of spontaneous and uncontrollable mirth at the sight of a stylish person in pursuit of his hat, which Boreas has snatched from its abiding place on its owner's head. I never could fathom what there is so very funny about the thing, though it is noticeable that the party in pursuit always "comes up smiling," and seems to rather enjoy his brief claim to public notice. There's nothing remarkable about it. Now if the hat was to be seen chasing its owner the case would be different. A stray hat is a fitting symbol of human life and aims. When we get a little wealth we enlarge the borders of our garments and deck ourselves with phylacteries. We wear our riches as the youth weareth his hat, and it is quite likely that the first gust of adversity which strikes us will send us in hot pursuit after our fleeting possessions, which seem always just out of our reach, like the *ignis-fatuus*, eluding our grasp again and again, while all the time we feel conscious of the undignified position we occupy, yet "smile and smile," and be a "heap mad" still. Don't be so foolish as to forsake the seashore even if it rains two days; it *can't* rain always, nor can the sun always shine upon you when you want it to do so.

Atlantic City.   Chapter XVIII.

The local history of Longport, although covering a period beginning much later than that of its big sister town to the north-east, furnishes a valuable record of foresight, perseverance and energy. Seventeen years ago, when Mr. M. S. McCullough, the founder of Longport, and its present mayor, first determined that he could and would transform the lonely desert of sand dunes into a pleasure community, there were (as there

The Borough of Longport

IN THE BAY

always are and always will be) many wiseacres who proclaimed their belief that things were already "over-done" upon the island; that Atlantic City had touched the high-water mark of its prosperity and greatness, and as for any new places, it was just so much money wasted to promote them. Despite these very common and fallacious opinions of the past, the sparkling city by the sea has spread amazingly, adding new attractions year after year, and so far from regarding the ambitions of Longport with a jealous eye she has leveled and beautified much of the intervening wastes, joined hands with Longport in the completion of a magnificent drive, unsurpassed upon the Atlantic coast, and by extending the electric railway to the south-west as far as Longport has made the younger resort practically her most important and promising suburb.

LOOKING SOUTHWEST AT LONGPORT

LOOKING NORTHEAST AT LONGPORT

The Longport driveway will be the great feature of development for the season of 1899. One-third of the cost of the new road will be paid by the State under the law for the development of better roads. Not only will it vastly stimulate the use of horses for both the saddle and carriage, and add greatly to the pleasure of cycling, but undoubtedly it will bring into service the new automobile type of carriage and thus develop a fashionable afternoon hour when all the world upon wheels will seek the new drive in endless review, a bright kaleidoscopic parade of wealth and style from the lighthouse to the crescent beach at Longport. *A Great Drive*

By electric cars, closed and heated in winter, open and breezy in summer, it is but a whirl of thirty minutes to or from Longport. By carriage it is less than one hour; the roar of the surf to the south-east and the calm waters of the bay upon the inland vista are charming features of this ride.

Do not cherish the delusion that when you have made the little journey upon the "trolley line" as far as the steamboat landing, you have seen Longport. As a matter of fact you have only just penetrated its suburbs.

Atlantic and Pacific avenues are bisected by the transverse avenues, and the whole is enclosed by Beach avenue, which, as its name indicates, borders the shore line not only along the sea front but around the shapely curve of Great Harbor Inlet and eastward along the bay to the landing, thus furnishing a superb finish to the splendid new drive already described.

Advantages   Having so many reasons for the most harmonious relations with the famous "city by the sea" existing as it were but next door to her, it would ill become Longport to indulge in comparisons at the expense of the older and greater resort, but there are one or two facts which may be safely mentioned. The first of these is in reference to the beautiful sloping beach which extends all the way around the point and far up the bay shore. There are no ragged edges of crumbling marsh; it is all clean sloping gravel and sand, and from whatever quarter the winds may blow there is always a stretch of shore where the wavelets ripple gently and where there is sunshine and comfort.

Apropos of another claim, it must be conceded that the future yachting interests, as well as the most popular fishing facilities, will be centred at Longport.

Mr. P. M. Sharples, who contributes a lively description of life at Longport in its many phases (see page 129), has touched upon this topic

ELECTRIC CAR STATION

convincingly. There is room in the bay for all the pleasure craft between New York and St. Augustine.

Beautiful Homes The accompanying illustrations indicate the artistic and substantial character of the residences which establish the class of Longport improvements. The lots are of liberal dimensions, and in some sections of the borough but one cottage is allowed upon a lot.

Having thus sketched the Longport of to-day we may consistently record as an important chapter in the history of the island the story of the

making of the settlement. In his first annual message addressed to the Longport Borough Council in April, 1898, Mayor M. S. McCullough furnished the substantial basis of fact upon which all future histories of the place must be built.

Mr. McCullough purchased the site of Longport from James Long of Philadelphia, in the year 1882, including the entire area from a line drawn between the present 23d and 24th avenues and Great Egg Harbor Inlet. It was an absolutely primitive waste. The first building was erected at 16th and Beach avenues and was used for a restaurant. It has since been moved to 17th and Atlantic avenues. The desolate sand hills reared their wind-swept crests everywhere. One of the greatest tasks in sight was the levelling of many of these in order to establish properly graded streets and building sites. The sand dunes were of such great height that from the location of the Aberdeen Hotel the thoroughfare could not be seen.

In his message Mr. McCullough says: "After careful study of the situation, noting the long hard and smooth beach along the ocean, the long port or harbor on the bay or thoroughfare, the close proximity of Atlantic City, the freedom from meadow land, the sand beach along the thoroughfare as well as along the ocean, the grand outlook over the sea as well as over the quiet waters of the thoroughfare and the bay, and the beautiful landscape beyond, it seemed to be an ideal place to found a family resort, and to make it attractive, as such, has since been my constant aim."

Building lots were offered for sale late in 1882, and in April, 1883, a special excursion train brought to Atlantic City a pleasant party of Philadelphians who were taken to Longport along the beach in carriages, and many of them became identified as real estate owners with the future destinies of the new settlement. It is a matter of much satisfaction to all concerned, and especially to the original promoter of the enterprise, that all of the rosy forecasts made upon that occasion have long ago been far more than realized.

The first cottage builders were Mr. Amos Dotterer and Mrs. S. L. Oberholtzer, the first locating at 17th and Beach avenues and the second at 19th and Beach avenues. Cottages were built by Prof. J. P. Remington and his sister, Miss Caroline Remington, in the spring of 1884. In the same year a Philadelphia caterer had charge of the restaurant, and so attractive was the place that the building, which is now the west wing of the Aberdeen, could not accommodate all who wished to come.

The first train of cars entered Longport on the morning of August 31st, 1884; prior to that time passengers were conveyed by carriage to and

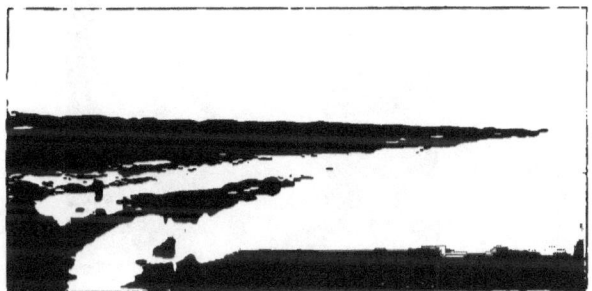

from south Atlantic City. In a few years, however, travel increased so rapidly that the Railroad Company put into service between Atlantic City and Longport small cars with steam motors, making frequent trips between the two places, and in 1893, introduced the present electric system. Among the events of 1884 was the organization of an Agassiz Association, the Oberholtzer family being the prime movers. The first meeting was held in their cottage. Much pleasure and benefit were derived from the study of natural history as found in the specimens of animals and algæ from the sea and wild flowers from the land, which were gathered and brought in for examination.

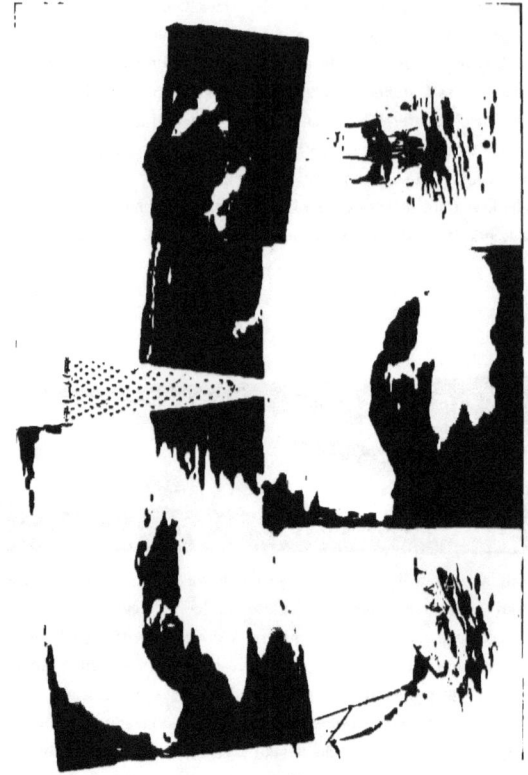

SAND DUNES NEAR LANGPORT

Interest in this society seemed to warrant a wider field than at first had been determined, and the present Longport Society of Natural Science was duly incorporated under the laws of New Jersey. The Society erected a hall at the corner of 15th and Atlantic avenues, which has been of great benefit to Longport, being used for divine worship on Sunday and for lectures and other purposes during the week.

Natural Science

In 1886 the Aberdeen was enlarged and leased to Mr. James Hood and Miss Elizabeth Newport; shortly after Mr. Hood having built the Pennhurst, in Atlantic City, Miss Ella Hood and Miss Elizabeth Newport assumed management of the Aberdeen. They were very successful, making many friends for themselves and also for Longport.

Hotels and Clubs

In 1890, Miss Hood being needed in the management of the Pennhurst, and Miss Newport unwilling to assume the entire charge of the Aberdeen, they reluctantly withdrew, and it was leased to Mr. James M. Moore, now proprietor of the Revere, Atlantic City.

The Aberdeen was under Mr. Moore's management during the seasons of 1890 and 1891. In the spring of 1892 Mr. Wilmer W. Lamborn, who associated with him Mrs. Elizabeth Kitts, purchased it, and under their management it has been enlarged, and many improvements have been made, and it has continued to grow in favor with the public.

In 1886 Mr. James Long erected a beautiful cottage and made it his summer residence until recently, when he sold it to Mr. A. H. Phillips and Mr. Carlton Godfrey. Also in 1886 the Bay View Club rented and occupied a house which had been built for them on 17th avenue. The members of the Club have taken great interest in Longport, and have done much for its improvement. They now own and occupy their new clubhouse, corner 17th and Beach avenues.

Mr. Fred Boice and sisters erected and opened the Devonshire in 1895, and have been very successful in its management. In 1896 Mr. A. H. Phillips, of Atlantic City, became interested in Longport and made large

VIEW FROM BAY LANDING

purchases of property for himself as well as for his friends, and has done much to improve the property he purchased. The beautiful residence he erected for his own use, and the one for Mr. R. M. Elliott are handsome additions to Longport. In addition to the cottages already named, others have been built by Elizabeth Newport, Philip M. Sharples, David Scott, Anna B. Hunter, Aaron B. Steelman, M. McCoy, Thos. S. Butler, Wilton D. Jackson, Mrs. James Sampson, Thos. C. Pearson, John R. Minnick, Samuel Stetzer, Bolton E. Steelman, Mrs. Henry Disston and M. S. McCullough.

The United States Government also erected a Life-Saving Station at the corner of 23rd and Atlantic avenues.

The pavilion at the foot of 16th avenue was built by the railroad company, and the restaurant connected with it has for some years been leased by Capt. James B. Townsend, who built a residence for himself, purchased the property at the corner of 17th and Atlantic avenues, and opened a store, which has been a great convenience to the residents. The Ferry

Longport and its neighbor, Ocean City, have been connected with the mainland at Somers' Point for many years by a ferry. The service which was formerly desultory, and at times rather nerve-trying, is now about as safe, speedy and comfortable as money and enterprise can make it. The Pennsylvania Railroad Company, which controls the trolley line between Longport and Atlantic City, maintains a service of fast steam yachts upon this route which are models of their kind. They are beamy and supplied with large seating capacity, being open all around the sides in fair weather, affording an unrestricted view. In wet, or cold weather, the sides are curtained. As elsewhere described, they form a part of a charming local round tour, the continuation from Somers' Point being by dummy train through Pleasantville and across the meadows back to Atlantic City.

In 1895 the Longport Water and Light Company was formed. Water is obtained in abundance from an artesian well. The flow is so abundant that for nine months in the year the surplus is utilized as power for pumping.

Much attention has been given to the important question of sanitation, and at the present time it is not too much to say that the drainage is nearly perfect. Borough Officials

The borough of Longport was created by act of Legislature, March 7th, 1898, and the following officers were elected April 5th, 1898 : Mayor, M. Simpson McCullough ; Councilmen, Arvine H. Phillips, Joseph P. Remington, Samuel Stetzer, Wm. H. Bartlett and John R. Minnick ; Assessor, Robert M. Elliott ; Collector, James B. Townsend; Justice of the Peace, J. P. Remington, Jr. ; Commissioners of Appeals in Cases of Taxation, Wilmer W. Lamborn, Bolton E. Steelman and J. P. Remington, Jr. Mr. Wilmer W. Lamborn was appointed Borough Clerk ; Carlton Godfrey, Borough Attorney ; John P. Ashmead, Borough Engineer ; M. McCoy, Superintendent of Highways, and Daniel Yates, Marshal.

More hotels and homes are to be the order of the early future. Broad areas still unoccupied will soon be well covered with pleasant avenues of cottages. New neighbors will bring new stimulus and still greater ambitions for the beautifying and comfort of this ideal spot. Nothing can halt the impetus of its steady progress. The fashion of a sojourn by the sea,

THE YACHT CLUB

once reserved for the wealthy, is now the privilege of all classes of citizens. It has become a necessity in the lives of vast numbers. To own and occupy a cottage by the ocean not only lends a wonderful zest to the otherwise monotonous lines of workers in the great cities, but is actually with many a real matter of economy. Longport is but an hour and a half from Philadelphia.

Seashore Joys The dweller by the sea knows a multitude of minor joys to which the people of the great cities are strangers. It is for him that the splendors of dawn gild the tossing blue expanse of the deep. For him only there is the quick appetizing walk along the beach before breakfast, the rare finds among the mass of flotsam and jetsam tossed up by the last high tide; for him the sea-bird's cry and the twitter of the meadow lark; for his appreciative eye the creamy sails along the bay, just spread to catch the first faint puff of the coming breeze, and his alone the romance of the ships that grow upon the far horizon and fade toward distant lands—the silent merchants of the deep. Neither mountains, inland lakes or broad rivers can give that ecstatic sense of life and happiness which is the daily stimulus of those who live upon the sands where the salt billows break and the breezes sing through the cedars.

The coming and going of the sun is brilliant and spectacular—a wondrous burst of color. The rise and decline of Luna is chaste and poetical. Taken together they form one of the grandest phases of nature, and nowhere are they seen more frequently in the perfection of their golden and silver drapery than at Longport.   *In Spring*

The vast majority of city people know the sea only in its midsummer aspects, but in every season it has its special charms. In the springtime there is the pleasure of watching nature as she responds to the soft blandishments of the balmy winds and ardent sunshine. The wide reaches of young marsh grass are of the most delicate green. Even the neglected sand dunes take on an emerald tinge. Everywhere is heard the cheerful

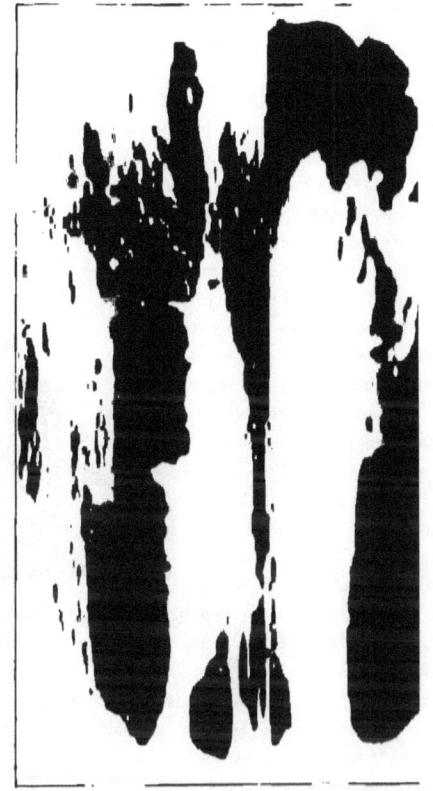

"WHERE THE SEA WAVES BREAK"

echo of the hammer and the rasp of the saw. Everywhere the painter spreads fresh color upon storm-worn surfaces. Everybody is busy making ready for the business of the summer. It is like youth when all the good things of life are yet in anticipation.

Autumn   Autumn has its own votaries. Then the gunner takes his innings. The myriads of wild fowl that swarm the creeks and thoroughfares of great Egg Harbor Bay have no rest. From skiff and blind and sneak-box the bang! bang! of the shot-gun is constant; and then, later, when the birds are gone, snow flurries sweep across the brown landscape and indigo sea, driving the all-the-year-round residents into the recesses of their cottages, and a new chapter in the life of the year begins. It is the holiday time of winter.

COTTAGE OF PROF. JOSEPH P. REMINGTON

Winter   Winter no longer stalks hand-in-hand with desolation through the empty avenues of a deserted city of pleasure. The great permanent population of Atlantic City has been elsewhere detailed. There is a brighter showing of stir and life there and at Longport than in most inland towns. The temperature as a rule is higher, and the temptations to healthful, joyous out-of-door life are more constant than in inland cities. Longport faces almost directly toward the south, and that accounts for much of its well-established reputation as a winter refuge.

It is certain that there is a large class of semi-rural people whose affairs drag them into the cities but now and then, and who have nothing in common with the farmer except to buy his surplus. These are the people who should be caught up by a beneficent fate and set down for the balance of their lives by the seashore, to write stories, paint, delve in hobbies or cut coupons, as the case may be, in a climate wonderfully exempt from those ills which make life in this latitude, between November and May, ordinarily a prolonged struggle for continued existence.

One of the most enthusiastic summer residents of Longport is Mr. P. M. Sharples, of West Chester, Pa.; a gentleman who, with his family, devotes the warmer half of the year about equally to the seashore and the Thousand Islands. At the request of the editor he has penned the following entertaining description of the joys of life upon the sands:

COTTAGE OF MR. P. M. SHARPLES

Joys of Longport

"It is feared that a description of the advantages and pleasures of Summer life at Longport will lead to the impression that the writer is either a hotel owner with a desire to boom that resort, or is the owner of property there which he is trying to sell. So let me preface these remarks with the statement that I am neither, but on the contrary would personally prefer to see the village remain just as it is.

An increase in population means less freedom, more conventionality, less sociability and more cosmopolitan surroundings.

At present the little town is just the right size, and each inhabitant has the feeling that he owns the whole place and can do in it as he would in his own back yard.

It is rare, indeed, that a home-like little seashore town should have such complete railroad facilities and the best markets in the land right at hand. Its proximity to Atlantic City, however, and the fact that every five minutes all day and well into the night a swift trolley car pulls right up at the back door gives Longport both.

In front of the house where this is written, not one hundred feet away, is the full unobstructed stretch of the finest bathing beach on the Atlantic coast, while but three hundred yards in the rear is a long and

AN AFTERNOON ON THE BAY

substantial fishing and sailing pier extending well out into the deep waters
of the thoroughfare.

The Thoroughfare

This thoroughfare, swarming in season with sea bass, black fish and weak fish, with an occasional sheepshead and plenty of small blue fish, opens at one extremity into Great Egg Harbor, as fine a sheet of inland yachting water as the coast affords, and in another direction leads to miles of smooth, safe water where crabbing and fishing can be indulged in with perfect safety during the roughest weather.

Miles of sailing in almost every direction from our pier can be indulged in by the fortunate owner of one of the beautiful, obedient and convenient, though illy named, "cat boats." Half an hour's sail in one direction brings us to oyster beds and oyster houses where the finest bivalves can be purchased for seventy-five cents per bushel, while in another direction the best fishing or crabbing is found.

Atlantic City is within sailing distance, while Ocean City is but one and a half miles in the opposite direction, and close alongside are Somers' Point and Pleasantville—all reached over inland waters safe to sail on at any time.

The Lower Inlet

Before reaching Ocean City, and less than a mile from our pier, is the "Inlet," opening right out into the broad ocean, so that when sea fishing and sailing are at their best no time is lost in getting right on to the fishing grounds with least delay.

This latter feature, lost sight of by many sojourners at the seaside, is one of the leading attractions to the writer when he is at Longport. The ocean fishing is at its best in September and October, and if I may be excused for expressing my opinion I will state that there are no other months half so enjoyable at the shore as those of September and October. The best bathing can be enjoyed throughout September, while, as stated, fishing and sailing are at their finest ; mosquitoes have departed, or are less rabid in their attacks ; the gunning is beginning to get interesting for those who indulge. The fishing and sailing continue into October and November; the air is something delightful, and the woods at Longport become beautiful. I know that even some of the inhabitants of Longport will exclaim that there are no woods, but nevertheless, within five or ten minute's walk from our house there is a beautiful stretch of woods, composed of holly trees with trunks a foot or more in diameter, large evergreens and aged oak trees. A walk through this woods in October is a treat. Bushels of luscious wild fox grapes and sprightly chicken grapes can be had for the

pulling, while great trees, covered with the red holly-berries or oaks with the drooping bitter-sweet, are at every side.

Before the end of September nearly all the Summer residents of Longport have departed, but " our house " is only a stone's throw from the United States life-saving crew, so we would never get lonely even in the middle of winter. These brave and experienced men of the ocean are kind and obliging to a degree. Rubber boots, gum coats, guns, and other requisites are gladly loaned to any of us who may be short of such supplies, and

MARINE ALGA
(LLANGPORT)

In Late Autumn

advice regarding the weather, as well as help in sailing or fishing make things especially interesting. Twice a week the life-saving apparatus is brought out and a most interesting drill takes place, including the throwing of a line to an imaginary wreck, and the saving of some one in the breeches buoy, besides practice in the breakers with the life-saving boat.

Now you think I have been all over the special attractions of Longport, but I have not, for there are yet to be extolled the cool breezes which always blow at Longport, though Atlantic City may be suffering with the heat; the purest artesian water, the bathing beach which slopes so gradually into the ocean and as hard as a board; the fleet of steamers sailing every few minutes, and for ten cents will take you a long cruise over Great Egg Harbor; besides the shell beach, the sand dunes, and the only sandy bay beach to be found on the coast. But it would require a volume to describe all these and others."

Atlantic City. Chapter XVIII.

    The numerous sea-coast beacons established and maintained by the national government along our coasts form both the most conspicuous and picturesque features of the immediate ocean front. Perched often upon lofty
Light-houses promontories or reared upon tempest-battered reefs, they attract the eye and appeal to the imagination with a force only exceeded by the sentiment awakened upon passing one of those restless outer guards of our land, the solitary light-ships. The models upon which our light-houses are constructed are of almost infinite variety, conforming to the location and desired range of light, as well as to the personal ideas of the engineers and board in charge.

    Light-houses for the guidance and warning of mariners are nearly as old as civilization. The first recorded light-house was the tower of Pharaoh, of Alexandria, built nearly three centuries before Christ. The oldest existing light-house is at Corunna, Spain. It was built in the reign of Trojan and
Antiquity reconstructed in 1634.
of Beacons The first beacon light upon our shores was maintained by the merchants of Boston at Allerton Point, where "fier-bales" were burned in an iron basket upon the top of a stone tower. In Boston harbor, too, was placed the first real light-house of the Atlantic coast in 1715-16 upon Little Brewster Island. It was erected at the expense of the Province.

    The control of the light-houses was assumed by the general government in 1789. At that time but one light, that of Sandy Hook, was

135

maintained within the State of New Jersey. This was established in the year 1762. The lights now maintained within the limits of Atlantic county are at Tucker Beach and Atlantic City (Absecon Light). The former guards the entrance into Little Egg harbor. It is distinguished by a black tower forty-six feet high upon top of a white dwelling with lead-colored trimmings and green shutters. Its location is eighteen miles southwest from Barnegat light and ten miles northeast from Absecon light. It shows a fixed white light varied by red flashes, the light showing white for one minute followed by six red flashes at intervals of ten seconds, visible twelve and one half miles.

A Moble Beacon

Absecon light, which is probably familiar to more people than any other light-house upon the Atlantic coast south of the Highlands, is set upon a shapely brick tower 159 feet high, having a broad, red band in the centre, the balance above and below being white. At its base are two white dwellings with lead-colored trimmings and green shutters facing upon Rhode Island Avenue. It shows a fixed white light, visible nineteen miles. It is distant from Barnegat light twenty-eight miles, and from Cape May light thirty-seven miles. This light was built in 1853 at a cost of $50,000. Thousands of visitors annually toil up its winding iron stairway to be rewarded at the top by a magnificent panorama of land and sea, all of the once desolate strips of sandy beach being dotted with a chain of beautiful summer resorts of more or less note, while in the foreground is peerless Atlantic City with its mile upon mile of beautiful streets and avenues ; its hundreds of hotels, countless stores, public buildings and private homes ; its unrivalled beach and magnificent Boardwalk ; its trio of railroads, and numerous heavy trains hurrying to and fro laden with pleasuring humanity ; its fleets of fairy-sail craft, and its great, happy population, temporary and permanent together, enlivening all of its open spaces, a scene which every old resident must gaze upon with a thrill of pride and every stranger view with wonder. The venturer who toils up the two hundred and twenty-

View from the Tower

eight steps of Absecon tower is interested, too, in the beautiful mechanism of the great lamp set in the midst of its prismatic Fresnel lantern. Just beneath and upon the level with the exterior gallery is the little watch-room in which the keeper holds nightly vigil. The post of light-house keeper was held for many years by genial Major "Abe" Wolf, long a familiar figure in the town. Many a stormy winter's night has the writer shared his watch and listened to his yarns, while the howling gale outside shook and swayed the great structure in which we sat, and the roar of the surf was incessant. The Major maintained intimate relations with scientists and sportsmen in the city, to whom he frequently sent fine specimens of aquatic fowl, and sometimes very rare birds which, flying with great force against the glass prisms, were easily picked up in a stunned condition upon the gallery or at the foot of the light-tower. The cats of the town were aware, with true feline intuition, just when the fat and toothsome birds were likely to fall, and very often deprived the Major of coveted specimens, and such was his antipathy for these nocturnal hordes that he sometimes snared them and sent them home minus their caudals; and it is estimated that during his incumbency the majority of the cats in Atlantic City possessed tails more or less abbreviated, and their descendants might well make claim to consanguinity with the famous cats of Manx. Fine specimens of brant and other strong flyers were to be seen domesticated among the Major's flocks of chickens and ducks.

The light-house is open in summer for visitors from 9 A. M. to noon, and in winter from 11 A. M. to noon, Sundays and stormy days excepted.

The following descriptions of lights and buoys in the vicinity of Atlantic City are obtained from official sources:

ABSECON
LIGHT

Little Egg Harbor Inlet

COAST AND GEODETIC SURVEY CHARTS 122 AND 8

SAILING DIRECTIONS.—Vessels intending to make this inlet will make the Outer Bay, and then run from buoy to buoy until opposite the Seventh, then NW. to anchorage. The channel of this inlet changes frequently. Every effort will be made to keep the buoys in the best water, but strangers should always exercise caution. There should be 4½ feet on the bar at low water.

Name of station or locality of aid	Color of aid	Number of buoy	Description of mark or aid	Compass bearings and distances of prominent objects from the aid	Depth at lowest tides, in ft.	GENERAL REMARKS. (NOTE.—Bearings and courses are magnetic, and distances expressed in nautical miles.)
Outer Buoy	Black and white perpendicular stripes		2d-class nun	Tucker Beach Light-House, NNE. ½ E. Little Beach Life-Saving Station, NNW. Second (or Bar) Buoy, N. by W., ¼ W.	14	
Second (or Bar) Buoy	Black and white perpendicular stripes		3d-class can	Third Buoy, N. by E. Tucker Beach Light-House, NNE.	17	
Third Buoy	Black and white perpendicular stripes		3d-class can	Tucker Beach Light-House, NE. by N. Fourth Buoy, N. ½ W.	24	In mid-channel
Fourth Buoy	Black and white perpendicular stripes		3d-class can	Fifth Buoy, N. ½ E. Tucker Beach Light-House, NE.	18	In mid-channel
Fifth Buoy	Black and white perpendicular stripes		3d-class can	Sixth Buoy, N. by E. ½ E. Tucker Beach Light-House, NE. by E. ½ E.	45	In mid-channel
Sixth Buoy	Black and white perpendicular stripes		3d-class can	Tucker Beach Light-House, E. Seventh Buoy, NW. by N.	45	In mid-channel
Seventh Buoy	Red		3d-class spar	Tucker Beach Light-House, E. by S. Eighth Buoy, W. by N.	11	This buoy stands on lower end of Middle Ground. Vessels must pass to the southward of it.
Eighth Buoy	Black and white perpendicular stripes		3d-class can	Tucker Beach Light-House, E. Absecon Light-House, SW. by S.	18	In mid-channel

138

Fifth Buoy	Red	3d-class nun	Absecon Light-House, S.	6	
Rum Point Day Beacon	Black and white.				Planted on Rum Point
		Large stake with five boards 5 feet long, placed at right angles			

Channel leading into Great Egg Harbor Inlet and Bay above Somers' Point.

(COAST AND GEODETIC SURVEY CHARTS 123 AND 8.

SAILING DIRECTIONS.—Vessels intending to enter this inlet, after making the outer (or Sea) Buoy, which lies just outside the bar, will steer from buoy to buoy. There should be 8 feet of water at low tide on the bar. The channel of this inlet changes frequently. Every effort will be made to keep the buoys in the best water, but strangers should always exercise caution.

Outer Buoy	Black and white perpendicular stripes	1st-class can	Great Egg Life-Saving Station, NNE. by E. Absecon Light-House, NE. ¾ E. Ocean City Life-Saving Station, NW. by N.	21	
Second (or Bar) Buoy	Black and white perpendicular stripes	2d-class nun	Absecon Light-House, NE. by E. Third Buoy, NNW.	12	
Third Buoy	Black and white perpendicular stripes	3d-class can	Absecon Light-House, ENE. Ocean City Life-Saving Station, SW. by W. Fourth Buoy, NW. by W.	18	In mid-channel
Fourth Buoy	Black and white perpendicular stripes	2d-class nun	Longport, E. by N. Fifth Buoy, W. by N.	4	In mid-channel, hard sandy bottom
Fifth Buoy	Black and white perpendicular stripes	3d-class spar	Ocean City Pier, SW. by S. Sixth Buoy, W. by S.	12	In mid-channel, hard sandy bottom
Sixth Buoy	Black and white perpendicular stripes	3d-class nun	Ocean City Pier, S. Seventh Buoy, WNW.	18	In mid-channel

Channel leading into Great Egg Harbor Inlet and Bay above Somers' Point.—Continued.

Name of station or locality of aid.	Number of buoy.	Color of aid.	Description of mark or aid.	Compass bearings and distances of prominent objects from the aid.	Depth at lowest tides, in ft.	GENERAL REMARKS. (NOTE.—Bearings and courses are magnetic, and distances expressed in nautical miles.)
Seventh Buoy		Black and white perpendicular stripes	3d-class can	Fish Factory, E. ½ N. Eighth Buoy, NW.	9	In mid-channel
Eighth Buoy		Black and white perpendicular stripes	3d-class nun	Absecon Light-House, NE. Wharf at Somers' Point, WNW.	12	In mid-channel
Ninth Buoy		Black and white perpendicular stripes	3d-class can	Bradford House, South Point, NE. by E. North Point Ocean City, SE. by E. Tenth Buoy, SW.	12	In mid-channel
Tenth Buoy		Black and white perpendicular stripes	3d-class can	North end of Ocean City Beach,ESE. ½ E. Eleventh Buoy, NNW.	24	In mid-channel
Eleventh Buoy		Black and white perpendicular stripes	3d-class spar	Beasley's Point Hotel, SSE. Twelfth Buoy, WNW.	29	In mid-channel
Twelfth Buoy		Black and white perpendicular stripes	3d-class can	Beasley's Point Hotel, SE. by S. Thirteenth Buoy, NW.	30	In mid-channel
Thirteenth Buoy		Black and white perpendicular stripes	3d-class nun	Bradford House, South Point, ENE. New Hotel, Beasley's Point, SE.	30	In mid-channel

ABOVE SOMERS' POINT.

Atlantic City. Chapter XIX.

The establishment of the Life-Saving Corps adjoins the light-house reservation. When the Atlantic City, or Absecon, light was established here the site was at a considerable distance from the surf line, but in later years the hook of sand which formerly extended outward upon the west side of the Inlet has been scoured away, and it was finally found needful to build jetties in front of the tower to keep the sea from undermining it.

The Life-Saving Service and Wrecks

As the Absecon beach is at a distance from the great havens to and from which the trans-Atlantic commerce plies it is but rare that great steamships come to grief upon this stretch of coast. The wreckage of vessels, both sail and steam, engaged in coastwise traffic is of frequent occurrence, and the eagle-eyed patrol located here holds a fine record for deeds of humanity and daring.

GIVING THE TOKEN

The original Government Boat-House at this point was opened about forty years ago, its first keeper being Ryan Adams, one of the early residents who came here in 1833. He was succeeded by Samuel Adams, and he, in turn, by Barton Gaskill who was the incumbent for sixteen years. In June, 1878, the station was removed to its present site upon Vermont avenue, near the light-house, Capt Amasa Bowen being appointed keeper. The building now in use was finished in 1884, and is one of the model stations of the coast. The first floor contains three rooms and a pantry, the second floor having three bed-rooms with a tower above where a constant watch is maintained for vessels which may need help. The crew consists of the keeper and seven men. The present keeper is Timothy H. Parker. The names of the crew are: I. S. Conover, Wm. B. Treux, Thos. R. Nixon, George Tomlinson, Joseph Holdscom, George Strickland and Henry Headley. The shore is patrolled at night by the guards in relief.

The Atlantic City Station

ALL READY

Upon the first clear day of each week the crew drills at 8 A. M. upon the beach, with mortar, life-line and surf-boat. The apparatus stored in the station is varied and interesting, and is explained courteously to visitors at any hour of the day.

The Atlantic City Life-Saving Station is one of thirty-nine located at nearly equally distant points upon the New Jersey coast, which is known as the Fourth District of the Life-Saving Service, the superintendent of which is located at Washington. The records of the service show that in the ten years between 1885 and 1894 inclusive (the most recent data at hand) the following was accomplished by the crews of the Fourth and Fifth Districts between Atlantic City and Chincoteague, Va.:

Statistics

Total number of casualties,	447
Property involved,	$6,135,325
Property saved,	$4,594,860
Persons on board,	2,671
Lives lost,	17

A competent authority has estimated that in the past seventy years upward of 500 ships have been lost upon Absecon beach, or within sight of it. When it is remembered that until the Life-Saving Service was insti-

142

tuted there was but little help to be had from the shore, the significance of the above report and the heroic work of this fearless body of public servants become more manifest.

Ship Ashore When the rumor goes forth, like a great electric thrill, from house to house and lip to lip all through the widespread city, be it summer or winter, that there is a wreck upon the shoals the beach is presently black with an excited, deeply interested throng. The myriad of occupants of the great brilliantly lighted hotels forsake the rich parlors and cafés for the Boardwalk, shivering with sympathetic apprehension as they watch the rockets gleaming momentarily far out in the tumultuous waste of waters, and see the red glare of the Coston torches as the life-boats speed away to the rescue. It is something well worth while to be in Atlantic City when a wreck comes in. It is rare, nowadays, that lives are lost upon this coast through disasters to ships, but in the course of a year, from one reason or another, unfortunate shippers lose their vessels along here, or are obliged to jettison a part of their cargo to get away from the dangerous shoals in front. When the alert town boys begin to throng up from the shore with bunches of bananas or boxes stenciled with foreign marks which look suspiciously like fine imported wines, it's high time to make a break for the beach and take a chance in the lottery of the sea, which sometimes rewards the patient searcher in a most magnificent fashion.

THE COSTON TORCH

Famous Wrecks Prior to the establishment of the Life-Saving Service along this coast no systematic record of wrecks was kept; the only data obtainable was to be found in the often unreliable pencilings of the older natives and their ancestors, scribbled upon the fly-leaves of old books, or existing in the traditions of the families who formerly gleaned considerable profit from the misfortunes of those who were cast upon this forlorn and inhospitable coast. There are tales without end of big ships which have been broken upon the bar and swept in piecemeals to litter the shore far and wide with twisted and

143

torn wreckage. One of the oldest of these local records refers to the wreck of the British transport *Mermaid*, at Egg Harbor Inlet in 1779, while bringing troops from Halifax, when 145 persons were drowned.

The wreck of the ship *Gherges Kahn* occurred in 1830. The majority of the passengers were saved, but Captain Busk, the commander, is said to have deliberately submitted to drowning rather than face the underwriters.

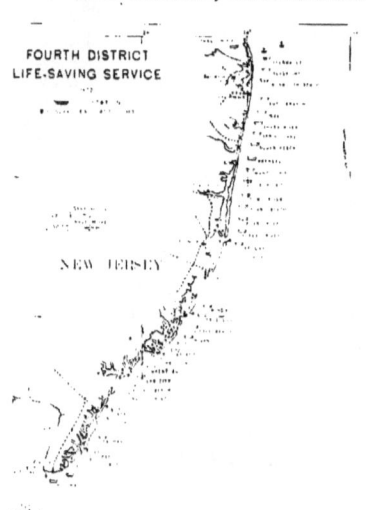

FOURTH DISTRICT
LIFE-SAVING SERVICE

NEW JERSEY

Soon afterward the *John Willetts* came ashore with some loss of life, and in 1845 the *Rainbow* was lost here. Upon Long Beach the brig *Patapsco* was lost in 1847, not far from the remains of the schooner *General Scott*, wrecked seven years earlier, whose captain was the only survivor. In 1856 the *Charles Colgate* came ashore at Long Beach, and two years later the *Flying Dutchman* drove in.

Upon Brigantine and Absecon shoals in 1847, '48 and '49 the schooners *Ann Nile*, *Ida*, *Walter A. Merchant*, *Brook Haven*, and barges *Chester* and *Mary Ellen* were lost. These disasters probably represent an average of the vast destruction of life and property upon this coast before the laggard authorities of the general government could be induced to light and patrol this dangerous sea-line, as, between 1847 and 1856, sixty-four vessels were lost here. The fearful wreck of the barque *Powhatan*, upon Long Beach, twenty-five miles north of Atlantic City, took place in 1854, when all of the passengers, mainly immigrants coming from Havre, with the crew, numbering in all 311 souls, perished. Nearly fifty bodies came ashore upon Absecon beach. Upon the same night the schooner *Manhattan* was lost at the same place, eight being drowned. Since the lighthouse was founded one of the worst wrecks was that of the *Santiago de Cuba* in 1867, upon Long Beach, which was attended by seven fatalities.

WATCHING THE CREW

One of the most curious wrecks which ever came upon the Atlantic City beach was that of the steamer *Rockaway*, a great excursion vessel, which was launched with much ceremony upon March 23, 1877; started in tow for New York harbor, and having broken away from the tug in a gale, broke her back upon the shoal and came upon the shore in front of the hotels in two parts, being driven so high that visitors could board her dry-shod at high tide.

Upon January 9, 1884, a fine, large, three-masted schooner, the *Robert Morgan*, of New Haven, came ashore at the foot of New York avenue, and five months later she was taken off with but little injury; although during her involuntary visit she was so high and dry that people could walk around her at low tide, and an admission price was charged to see her decks and interior.

THE ROBERT MORGAN

The Love Letter

Among the thronging memories of far away winter nights spent upon the tumultuous beach with the men of the coast guard there comes to the writer the thought of a letter rescued by him from a mass of drift two days after one of the most fearful wrecks ever known upon the Atlantic coast, and which gave occasion for these lines :

HER LETTER.

We walked at night the wreck-strewn sand,
  We walked and watched the dying storm ;
With eager eye and ready hand
  We sought to find some sea-tossed form.

And as we walked, the guard and I,
  The tide crept out till broad and gray
The shingled sand lay smooth and dry,
  Beneath our fitful lantern's ray.

On either side and everywhere
  Lay limp and broken bits of wreck,
Of clothing, ropes, of wooden ware—
  All kind of things one finds on deck.

From out this scattered wreckage waste
  I stopped and picked a little note ;
A dainty monogram was traced
  Above the lines the owner wrote :

" My darling," but it gave no name,
  As if he only of mankind
To such sweet title had a claim ;
  The words were coined her love to bind.

'Twas written full, and crossed again,
  All interlined with afterthought ;
'Twas spotted o'er with salter stain
  Than e'en the sea could yet have wrought.

" My darling ; " there a fold was pressed,
  The words just here were fainter yet,
As though 'twere worn upon his breast,
  A prized and sacred amulet.

Anon, she wrote her hopes and fears,
  Of fickle fortune's smile or frown,
Of homelike joys in coming years,
  When they were wed and "settled down."

She spoke of spring and Easter flowers,
  Of silk and satin for her bonnet,
Of sick friends, funerals, marriage dowers,
  Her new suit and the trimmings on it.

And so this unknown maiden wrote
  Her loving letter to its end,
And little dreamed the waves would float
  Her writing to a stranger's hand.

Somewhere, to-night, a girlish face
  Is raised to God in mute despair;
Somewhere a woman prays for grace
  And strength of soul her load to bear.

Somewhere along the wintry coast
  Her hopes lie buried in the sand,
While this tells of the love that's lost—
  This sea-stained letter in my hand.

F. H. T.

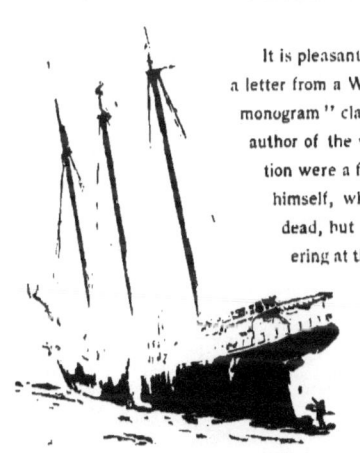

A WINTER
VICTIM

It is pleasant to relate that after a time there came a letter from a Western town bearing the same "dainty monogram" claiming the stray love-missive from the author of the verses, and beneath the maiden's petition were a few nervous lines from the young officer himself, who had been dragged from the surf as dead, but who was, at the writing, slowly recovering at the home of his boyhood. "And so they were married," and this little true story of the sea turns out just as things should, but seldom do.

And then there was the bottle

found rolling up and down the sand in the shallows which held a pretty message from a romantic little maiden away up the coast at Asbury Park, who hoped that her venture, which had been adrift now half a year, would come to some handsome youth in a far-off land, and that he would lose no time in his response. Alas! little maiden; it was picked up by a middle-aged man with a family, who printed it in a newspaper and sent you a marked copy as a warning.

The Message in a Bottle

IRON SHIPS
BREAK SLOWLY

The publishers of this work take pleasure in stating that in its preparation they have been supplied with the following complete data in regard to the various marine casualties which have occurred upon this coast since the Life-Saving Service was instituted, by General Superintendent, S. J. Kimball, of Washington. As a record for future reference this list will doubtless prove one of the most valuable features of this publication:

List of Casualties to Vessels

Which have occurred within the scope of the operations of the Life-Saving Stations, located in Atlantic County, Coast of New Jersey, from November, 1871 to June 30, 1897. It is a noteworthy fact that in not a single instance was there loss of life.

Date	Rig and Name	Tonnage	Locality	Estimated value of property involved	Estimated value of property saved	Estimated value of property lost	Number of persons on board
1871—November 25	Sc. Ware	395	Absecon Beach	$ 3,500	$ 3,500		6
1872—November 16	Sc. Alfred W. Fiske	34	Brigantine Beach	27,500	$27,000	$ 500	7
1873—August 23	Sc. Vht. Mary McCabe	258	South Brigantine Beach	4,000	4,000		12
1874—November 14	Sc. Ella Amsden	63	Brigantine Beach and Shoals	17,140		17,140	7
January 10	Sc. Atlantic	40	Brigantine Beach and Shoals	4,000	6,000		4
January 18	Sc. Seabird	435	Brigantine Beach and Shoals	6,000	4,000		4
March 29	Sc. Kate C. Rich	1000	Brigantine Beach and Shoals	20,000	20,000		8
April 16	Str. Nederland	425	Brigantine Beach and Shoals	700,000	675,000	25,000	60
May 13	Sc. Northern Light	240	Brigantine Beach and Shoals	10,000		10,000	6
1875—November 1	Sc. West Wind	29	Absecon Beach	4,500	4,200	300	6
February 3	Sc. Brandywine	168	Absecon Beach	23,000		22,000	9
September 2	Sc. R. J. Corson	262	Brigantine Beach	16,000	16,000		7
November 15	Sc. Elizabeth W. Godfrey	58	Absecon Bar	2,650	2,000	600	4
1876—January 10	Vht. N. King	5	Brigantine Inlet	1,000	1,000		2
May 14	Sc. Benjamin Franklin	75	Absecon Bar	3,705	3,765		6
1877—February 18	Sc. Mary Standish	400	Brigantine Shoals	1,010	910	100	7
August 13	Str. Richmond	2000	Brigantine Shoals	200,000	200,000		47
November 18	Slp. W. W. Wallace	15	Absecon Bar	560	560		2
1878—January 6	Sc. B. N. Hawkins	395	Brigantine Beach	23,000		23,000	1
January 26	Sc. Twilight	479	Brigantine Beach	85,000		85,000	11
January 30	Sc. Annie S. Carll	75	Absecon Bar	400	400		5
November 2	Sc. Dick Williams	175	Little Egg Harbor Bar	10,000	4,900		7
December 4	Bk. Wilhelmina	604	Little Egg Harbor Bar	7,950	6,925	75	14
December 6	Sc. Asenath A. Shaw	557	Brigantine Beach	43,000	40,500	2,500	8
December 20	Sc. J. B. Van Dusen	222	Brigantine Beach	11,000	10,790	210	5
December 24	Sc. C. and C. Brooks	135	Little Egg Harbor Bar	2,435		2,435	5
1879—June 21	Slp. John Leach	75	Little Egg Harbor Bar	2,500	2,500		5
June 27	Sc. Lydia Budd	50	Absecon Bar	1,920		1,920	6

149

List of Casualties Continued.

Date	Rig. and Name	Tonnage	Locality	Estimated value of property involved	Estimated value of property saved	Estimated value of property lost	Number of persons on board
July 8	Sc. Lydia B.	30	Absecon Bar	$1,600	$1,600		2
August 19	Sc. Flora Curtis	83	Brigantine Inlet	8,500	8,000	500	4
October 11	Bk. Antoinetta Costa	618	Brigantine Beach	30,000	20,000	10,000	14
October 17	Bk. Cutelin Ball Orso	634	Absecon Beach	20,000	15,000	5,000	14
November 5	Sc. Nellie Brown	281	Little Egg Harbor Shoals	6,335		6,335	7
1880—January 8	Sc. A. H. Quimby	68	Absecon Bar	7,000	7,000		5
January 28	Sc. May Montayne	28	Great Egg Harbor Bar	4,000	3,900	100	4
September 4	Sc. James S. Hewitt	204	Absecon Bar	16,000	14,500	500	6
October 13	Slp. Liddie Jones	13	Brigantine Shoals	875	700	175	2
December 2	Slp. William Tell	24	Absecon Bar	1,200	1,200		3
1881—December 30	Sc. George W. Rogers	42	Absecon Bar	1,800	1,800		5
January 6	Slp. Anson Stinson	224	Absecon Bar	35,000		35,000	7
February 2	Slp. John Roach	30	Absecon Bar	2,200	50	2,150	8
March 26	Sc. W. D. Cargill	295	Brigantine Shoals	19,000	18,400	600	8
April 3	Sc. L. F. Whitmore	441	Brigantine Shoals	5,800	5,800		4
August 15	Slp. Julia A. Reid	11	Absecon Bar	1,000	1,000		12
1882—September 24	Sc. Hattie J.	30	Great Egg Harbor Bar	900	400	500	3
September 24	Sc. J. and C. Merritt	34	Great Egg Harbor Bar	5,000	4,950	50	3
October 22	Sc. George Ankerson	8	Great Egg Harbor Bar	300	300		7
January 2	Sc. W. C. Wickham	330	Brigantine Shoals	50,000	50,000		6
April 22	Sc. Maggie Ellen	217	Brigantine Shoals	9,800	9,800		5
August 28	Sc. Estella Day	228	Absecon Bar	15,000	15,000		8
September 15	Slp. Alert	7	Absecon Bar	890	890		3
September 16	Slp. William Tell	25	Absecon Bar	1,000	1,000	10	2
November 3	Slp. L. C. Wallace	17	Absecon Bar	1,025	1,025		3
December 29	Slp. William Tell	25	Absecon Bar	830	300	530	
1883—January 11	Slp. Millie	20	Absecon Bar	1,000	200		17
January 12	Sc. Mary Ella	8	Great Egg Harbor Inlet	1,020	1,020		3
January 18	Sch. Fred. E. Scammell	1350	Brigantine Shoals	100,000	74,900	25,100	5
February 17	Sc. Enterprise	22	Absecon Bar	1,385		1,385	
September 26	Sc. M. B. Mahoney	139	Brigantine Shoals	4,300	4,225	75	

150

December 15	Slp. Kate Becker	7	Absecon Bar	$800	$775	$25	2
1884—January 4	Brig Alida A. Smith	181	Brigantine Shoals	17 000	17 000		8
January 6	Sc. John Anna	29	Great Egg Harbor Inlet	1 600	1 600		4
January 9	Sc. Robt. Morgan	553	Absecon Beach	40 000	39 000	1 000	9
March 7	St. Sp. Clyssdale	608	Brigantine Shoals	40 000	40 000		27
March 11	Str. Wm. Spicer	44	Great Egg Harbor Inlet	5 150	600	4 550	2
March 16	Slp. Vienna	21	Little Egg Harbor Shoals	1 250		1 250	6
April 9	Sc. George White	42	Great Egg Harbor Inlet	2 450	1 600	850	4
April 29	Sc. Florence L. Lockwood	284	Brigantine Shoals	9 100	9 040	60	6
May 17	Sc. William Tice	191	Absecon Bar	6 000	6 000		5
July 5	Sc. Annie M. Reynolds	61	Great Egg Harbor Inlet	5 950	5 900	50	5
November 6	Brig Mary E. Pennell	252	Brigantine Shoals	20 000	20 000		10
1885—January 2	Sc. Emma	8	Great Egg Harbor Inlet	300	300		4
February 11	St. Sp. Salisbury	1278	Brigantine Shoals	125 000	125 000		26
March 13	Slp. Golden Light	16	Absecon Bar	1 000	1 000		
August 14	Sc. Angie Predmore	94	Absecon Bar	4 500	900	3 600	6
November 10	Sc. Oliver H. Booth	243	Great Egg Harbor Inlet	10 320	9 600	720	7
November 11	Str. Absecon	53	Absecon Bar	10 150	7 650	2 500	13
December 26	Sc. Wm. E. Hewlett	23	Absecon Bar	1 500	1 500		3
1886—January 11	Sc. Mary S. Roundy	11	Absecon Bar	1 475	75	1 400	5
January 19	Sc. Georgiana	12	Absecon Bar	1 000	1 000		3
January 20	Slp. Eugene Seabright	19	Absecon Bar	600		600	
January 20	Slp. Idlewild	10	Absecon Bar	620	620		2
January 21	Sp. Georgiana	12	Absecon Bar	1 000		1 000	3
February 4	Slp. Alert	7	Absecon Bar	1 000	1 000		2
February 25	Slp. Flash	9	Absecon Bar	1 200	1 200		3
February 26	Sc. Edward M. Hartshorn	29	Absecon Bar	1 530	1 530		4
April 22	Slp. Emma	5	Little Egg Harbor Inlet	550	550		2
July 3	Sc. Sylvan Glen	22	Absecon Bar	1 500		1 500	4
July 3	Sc. Melody	22	Absecon Bar	2 000	1 600	400	3
July 21	Sc. Lizzie	86	Absecon Bar	3 500	3 255	245	4
August 7	Sc. Henry Disston	42	Absecon Bar	3 000	3 000		4
August 8	Sc. Banvard	168	Brigantine Shoals	2 000	1 850	150	6
October 7	Sc. John W. Fox	82	Absecon Bar	8 500	8 460	40	5
October 17	Sc. Hannah M. Buell	291	Absecon Bar	6 500	840	5 660	7
November 6	Sc. J. and H. Scull	111	Absecon Bar	8 500	8 475	25	5
1887—January 20	Sc. Annie E. Fowler	17	Absecon Bar	1 500	1 500		4
March 31	Sc. Cornelia Soule	306	Absecon Bar	17 400	7 200	10 200	6
July 26	Sc. Edward M. Hartshorn	29	Absecon Bar	2 700	2 500	200	5
October 22	Sc. Hannah Champion	75	Absecon Bar	2 800	2 750	50	4
1888—February 6	Sc. Gardner Colby	1077	Brigantine Shoals	11 700	11 675	25	4
March 12	Slp. Neptune	7	Absecon Inlet	600	400	200	

List of Casualties—Continued.

Date	Rig and Name	Tonnage	Locality	Estimated value of property involved	Estimated value of property saved	Estimated value of property lost	Number of persons on board
May 2	Sc. Sam'l L. Russell	194	Absecon Inlet	$5,000	$5,000		5
May 9	Slp. Greenwood	15	Absecon Inlet	2,100	2,100		2
May 14	Slp. John W. Fox	82	Absecon Inlet	6,600	6,600		5
August 14	Sc. Eva I. Shenton	92	Absecon Inlet	6,300	6,180	120	5
December 5	Sc. A. H. Quinby	68	Absecon Inlet	3,000	3,000		5
December 22	Sc. Annie S. Carll	48	Absecon Inlet	3,000	2,500	500	7
1889—January 5	Sc. Annie Godfrey	18	Absecon Inlet	880	715	165	3
March 24	Str. George Law	415	Absecon Bar	25,000	25,000		72
April 2	Slp. J. W. Luce	22	Absecon Bar	550	350	200	3
April 25	Sc. Louisa B. Robinson	30	Absecon Bar	4,000	4,000		3
August 2	Sc. Louisa B. Robinson	30	Great Egg Harbor Inlet	3,120	2,595	525	3
August 23	Sc. Henry B. Winship	497	Brigantine Shoals	10,450	10,440	10	13
September 2	Barkentine Nicanor	453	Great Egg Harbor Inlet	205,000	205,000		12
September 10	Sc. Palestine	31	Great Egg Harbor Inlet	1,450	1,410	40	5
November 30	Sc. Three Brothers	142	Great Egg Harbor Inlet	4,300	4,300		6
November 30	Sc. John W. Hall, Jr.	193	Absecon Inlet	3,900	3,900		7
December 20	Sc. Hattie Baker	346	Brigantine Shoals	9,200	9,200		6
1890—June 2	Bk. Stafford	156	Absecon Beach	1,000	1,000		7
1891—May 31	Sc. Commodore	26	Absecon Bar	28,000	28,000		3
August 18	Vht. Ida	27	Absecon Bar	7,000	6,800	200	7
December 11	Sc. Henry M. Clarke	173	Absecon Inlet	6,000	6,000		7
December 19	Sc. Annie Godfrey	18	Absecon Inlet	100	100		3
1892—February 5	Sc. Benj. B. Church	513	Brigantine Shoals	14,800	14,235	565	7
June 5	Sc. Sh. Venezuela	2893	Brigantine Shoals	850,000	850,000		72
June 16	Sc. Annie E. Fowler	17	Absecon Inlet	200	100	100	2
September 2	Sc. Arthur	56	Great Egg Harbor Inlet	5,000	5,000		4
1893—March 2	Sc. Marcia S. Lewis	347	Great Egg Harbor Inlet	5,700	5,000	700	6
March 7	Barkentine Baldwin	800	Brigantine Shoals	8,800	8,050	750	9
May 4	Sc. Edward M. Hartsdorn	29	Absecon Bar	200		200	3
July 29	Sc. Booth Brothers	348	Brigantine Shoals	17,000		17,000	8
	Vht. J. O. Smith	18	Absecon Inlet	2,500	2,500		9

152

Date	Vessel	No.	Location	Value	Value	Lives
August 24	Slp. C. S. Farnell	10	Absecon Inlet	$1 000	$1 000	1
September 2	Slp. Mascot	14	Absecon Inlet	1 800	1 800	40
October 24	Sc. John W. Fox	82	Absecon Inlet	5 000	5 000	4
October 26	Sc. Ethel	148	Absecon Inlet	9 800	9 785	5
November 16	Sc. Allie B. Cathrall	109	Absecon Inlet	5 750	5 750	5
November 24	Sc. John W. Fox	82	Absecon Inlet	5 500	5 500	4
December 11	Sc. Allie B. Cathrall		Absecon Inlet	5 850	5 850	5
December 27	Sc. Lizzie Bell	104	Absecon Inlet	2 050	2 050	5
1894—January 22	Str. Anide	41	Little Egg Harbor Inlet	300 000	283 000	42
June 25	Str. Bramble	1711	Little Egg Harbor Inlet	45 000	45 000	25
July 10	Sc. Katie G., Robinson	1508	Brigantine Shoals	5 000	4 000	5
September 1	Sc. Mary Ella	299	Absecon Inlet	1 100	1 060	2
September 10	Vht. Patrol	29	Absecon Inlet	3 000	2 975	$15 1
October 7	Str. Goldsboro	681	Little Egg Harbor Inlet	32 000	32 000	16
October 28	Sc. Sunbeam	22	Little Egg Harbor Inlet	1 050	1 050	2
November 12	Str. Wm. H. Davenport	250	Absecon Bar	17 500	17 500	6
1895—February 24	Str. Ben Bellido	1914	Brigantine Shoals	100 000	100 000	27
March 23	Sc. Vigilant	8	Little Egg Harbor Inlet	400	400	
May 9	Sc. John Anna	29	Great Egg Harbor Inlet	650	650	
May 11	Sc. Mary Ella	20	Absecon Inlet	800	370	2
May 13	Sc. Centennial	113	Absecon Inlet	3 810	3 800	3
August 10	Sc. E. Waterman	107	Absecon Inlet	9 000	9 000	3
October 9	Sc. H. B Metcalf	160	Absecon Inlet	6 250	400	6
October 9	Vht. Mary Atchison		Great Egg Harbor Inlet	550	550	4
October 30	Vht. Fenty		Absecon Inlet	300	295	3
October 31	Sc. Edith	498	Brigantine Beach	10 500	1 500	2
November 3	Str. E. F. C. Young	113	Absecon Beach	6 000	6 000	6
November 27	Str. F. P. Sov	10	Absecon Bar	3 000	3 000	5
1896—February 6	Sc. Asenath A. Shaw	557	Brigantine Beach	20 000	20 000	9
March 15	Sc. Thos. Thomas	44	Absecon Bar	2 300	2 300	7
April 4	Slp. Helen F. Leaming	361	Little Egg Harbor Inlet	16 000	16 000	5 $5
April 10	Sc. Palestine	15	Absecon Inlet	200	200	2
May 3	Slp. C. E. Wohl	31	Great Egg Harbor Inlet	500	50	3
September 12	Sc. Annie E. Fowler	13	Absecon Bar	1 000	1 000	30 $9 000
September 19	Sc. Ella R. Simpson	17	Absecon Bar	200	200	
November 15	Sc. Hattie Rebecca	83	Little Egg Harbor Inlet	3 000	3 000	4
December 4	Sc. Gertrude T. Browning	86	Absecon Bar	500	450	7 $50 3
1897—January 27	Sp. Francis	134	Absecon Bar	13 000	13 000	6
May 8		2077	Little Egg Harbor Inlet	300 000	37 500	262 500 25

153

List of Life-Saving Stations.

Names and Localities of Life-Saving Stations in Atlantic County, Coast of New Jersey, and the names of persons who have served as keepers of stations.

Designations of Stations since June 1, 1883	Localities	Year when Station was Erected	Number by which Stations were designated at different periods			Names of Keepers
			1849	1854	1872	
Little Beach	South Side Little Egg Inlet	1872			No. 24	Joseph P. Shourds William F. Gaskill Major B. Ireland Charles H. Horner James Rider
Brigantine	5½ miles north of Absecon Light	1849	No. 9	No. 18	No. 25	James Scull William Holdzkom John H. Turner Constant Brown James A. Abrams John M. Holdzkom
South Brigantine	3⅛ miles north of Absecon Light	1872			No. 26	C. A. Holdzkom William Holdzkom
Atlantic City	At Absecon Light	1849	No. 10	No. 19	No. 27	Samuel Adams Barton Gaskill Purnell Bowen Amasa Brown Timothy H. Parker
Absecon	2½ miles south of Absecon Light	1872			No. 28	Thomas Rose William W. Eldridge Israel S. Blackman Joseph L. Gaskill
Great Egg Harbor	6½ miles south of Absecon Light	1854		No. 20	No. 29	Joseph Ireland Japhet Townsend John Bryant Wm. H. Smith Levi P. Casto

154

Absecon Inlet and Bay above Anchorage to Brigantine Wharf.

Coast and Geodetic Survey Charts 122 123, and 8.

SAILING DIRECTIONS.—Vessels intending to enter this inlet should make the Sea Buoy, which lies just outside the bar; hard sandy bottom. From it steer from buoy to buoy. There is about 5 feet at low water on the bar. Every effort will be made to keep the buoys in the best water; but the channel is liable to changes, and strangers should exercise caution.

Name of station or locality of aid.	Color of aid.	Number of aid, if a buoy.	Description of mark or aid.	Compass bearings and distances of prominent objects from the aid.	Depth at lowest tides, in ft.	General Remarks. (Note.—Bearings and courses are magnetic, and distances expressed in nautical miles.)
Outer (or Sea) Bell Buoy	Black and white perpendicular stripes		Nun shaped with lattice body; bell rung by a ball rolled by action of the sea	South Brigantine Life-Saving Station, NNE. ¾ E. Absecon Light-House, NW. ¼ N. Second Buoy, NNW.	21	This buoy lies just outside of the bar. Pilots and masters of vessels are requested to notify the Light-House Inspector if this buoy drifts from its position or does not work satisfactorily.
Second (or Bar) Buoy	Black and white perpendicular stripes		2d-class nun	Absecon Light-House, NW. by W. Third Buoy, NNW.	8	Hard sandy bottom
Third Buoy	Black and white perpendicular stripes		3d-class can	Absecon Light-House, WSW. Fourth Buoy, N. by W.	9	In mid-channel
Absecon Light-Station	White and red horizontal bands; lantern white		Tower, 169 ft. high; lower third, white; middle third, red; and upper, white. Two white dwellings with lead-colored trimmings and green shutters	Barnegat Light-House, 28 miles Cape May Light-House, 37 miles		Fixed white light, visible 19 miles. On the south side of Absecon Inlet, Atlantic City, N. J. There is a life-saving station here.
Fourth Buoy	Black and white perpendicular stripes		3d-class can	South Brigantine Life-Saving Station, ENE. Absecon Light-House, S. To anchorage, NNW.	10	In mid-channel

155

Atlantic City.   Chapter XX.

Aboriginal Footprints

Dr. Charles C. Abbott, an ardent naturalist, has wandered much along this coast, and the following extracts from an essay born of his pen may well have place in the lore of the region.

"A ponderous geologist, with weighty tread and weightier manner, brought his foot down upon the unoffending sod and declared, 'These meadows are sinking at a rapid rate; something over two feet a century.' We all knew it, but Sir Oracle had spoken, and we little dogs did not dare to bark.

Not long after I returned alone to these ill-fated meadows and began a leisured, all-day ramble. They were very beautiful. There was a wealth of purple and of white boneset and iron weed of royal dye. Sunflower and primrose gilded the hidden brooks, and every knoll was banked with rose-pink centaury. Nor was this all. Feathery reeds towered above the marsh, and every pond was empurpled with pontederia and starred with lilies. Afar off acres of nut-brown sedge made fitting background for what meadow tracts were still green and grassy, while close at hand, more beautiful than all, were struggling growths held down by the golden dodder's net that overspread them.

It does not need trees or rank shrubbery to make a wilderness. This low-lying tract, to-day, with but a summer's growth above it, is as wild and lonely as the Western plains. Lonely, that is, as man thinks, but not forsaken. The wily mink, the pert weasel, the musk-rat and meadow mouse ramble in safety through it. The great blue heron, its stately cousin, the snowy egret, and the dainty bittern find it a congenial home.

An Indian Home

The fiery dragonfly darts and lazy butterflies drift across the blooming waste; bees buzz angrily as you approach; basking snakes bid you defiance. Verily, this is wild life's domain and man is out of place. It was not always so. The land is sinking, and what now of that older time when it was far above its present level—a high, dry, upland track along which flowed a clear and rapid stream? The tell-tale arrow point is our guide, and wherever the sod is broken we have an inkling of Indian history. The soil, as we dig a little deeper, is almost black with charcoal dust, and it is evident that, centuries ago, the Indians were content to dwell here, and well they might. Even in Colonial days the place had merit, and escaped not the eager eyes of Penn's grasping followers. It was meadow then, and not fitted for his house, but the white man built his barn above the ruins of his dusky predecessor's home. All trace of human habitation now is gone, but the words of the geologist kept ringing in my ears, and of late I have been digging. It is a little strange that so few traces of the white man are found as compared with relics of the Indian. From the barn that once stood here and was long ago destroyed by a flood it might be expected to find at least a rusty nail.

The ground held nothing telling of a recent past, but was eloquent of the distant long ago. Dull, indeed, must be the imagination that cannot recall what has been by the aid of such material as the spade here brought to light. Not only were the bow and spear proved to be the common

Reading the Past

weapons of the time, but there were in even greater abundance, and of many patterns, knives to flay the game. It is not enough to merely glance at a trimmed flake of flint or carefully chipped splinter of argillite, and say to yourself, 'a knife.' Their great variety has a significance that should not be overlooked. The same implement could not be put to every use for which a knife was needed; hence the range in size from those of several inches in length to tiny flakes that will likely remain a puzzle as to their purpose. It is supposed and possibly asserted that the Indian knew nothing of forks, but that he plunged his fingers into the boiling pot or held in his bare hands the steaming joints of bear or venison is quite improbable. Now, the archæologist talks glibly of bone awls whenever a sharpened splinter of bone is presented to him, as if only to perforate leather were such implements intended. They doubtless had other uses, and I am sure more than one split and sharpened bone that was found would have served excellently well as a one-tined fork wherewith to lift from the pot a bit of meat. Whether or not such forks were in use, there were wooden spoons, as a bit of a bowl and mere splinter of the handle served to show. Kalm tells us they used the laurel for making this utensil, but I fancied my fragment was hickory. Potsherds everywhere spoke of the Indians feasting, and it is now known that besides bowls and shallow dishes of ordinary sizes, they had huge vessels also, of several gallons' capacity. All these are broken now, but, happily, fragments of the same dish are often found together, and so we can reconstruct them."

But what did the Indians eat? Quaint old Gabriel Thomas, writing about 1696, tells us that "they live chiefly on *Maze* or *Indian Corn* rosted in the Ashes, sometimes beaten boyl'd with Water, called *Homine*. They have cakes, not unpleasant; also Beans and Pease, which nourish much, but the Woods and Rivers afford them their provision; they eat morning and evening, their Seats and Tables on the ground."

What Did They Eat?

In a great measure this same story of the Indians' food supply was told by the scattered bits found mingled with the ashes of an ancient hearth. Such fireplaces or cooking sites were simple in construction, but no less readily recognized as to their purpose. A few flat pebbles had been brought from the bed of the river near by and a small paved area, some two feet square, was placed upon or very near the surface of the ground. Upon this the fire was built, and, in time, a thick bed of ashes accumulated. Just how they cooked can only be conjectured, but the discovery of very thick clay vessels and great quantities of fire-cracked quartzite pebbles leads to the conclusion that water was brought to the boiling point by heating the stones to a red heat and dropping them into the vessel holding the water. Thomas, as we have seen, says corn was "boyl'd with water." Meat also was, I think, prepared in the same manner. Their pottery probably was poorly able to stand such harsh treatment, which would explain the presence of such vast quantities of fragments of clay vessels. Of traces of vegetable food none are now to be found, except very rarely. A few burnt nuts, a grain or two of corn, and, in one instance, what appeared to be a charred crab apple completes the list of what as yet have been picked from the mingled earth and ashes. This is not surprising, and what we know of vegetable food in use among the Delaware Indians is almost wholly derived from those early writers who were present at their feasts. Kalm mentions the roots of the golden club, arrow leaf and groundnut, besides various berries and nuts. It is well known that extensive orchards were planted by these people. It may be added that, in all probability, the tubers of that noble plant, the lotus, were used as food. Not about these meadows, but elsewhere in New Jersey this plant has been growing luxuriantly since Indian times.

A Lotus Land

Turning now to the consideration of what animal food they consumed, one can speak with absolute certainty. It is clear that the Delawares were meat eaters. It needs but little digging on any village site to prove this, and from a single fireplace, deep down in the staff soil of this sinking meadow, have been taken bones of the elk, deer, bear, beaver, rac-

A List of Game coon, muskrat and gray squirrel. Of these the remains of deer were largely in excess, and as this holds good of every village site I have examined, doubtless the Indians depended more largely upon this animal than upon all the others. Of the list only the elk is extinct in the Delaware Valley, and was probably rare even at the time of the European settlement of the country, except in the mountain regions. If individual tastes varied as they do among us we have certainly sufficient variety here to have met every fancy. Not one of the animals named but is considered eatable among ourselves, although raccoon is scarcely a delicacy. Eyebrows may raise at the suggestion of dining on muskrats; but he who has had their hind legs properly cooked, knows what a royal dish they make. Prominent among the bird-bones were those of the wild turkey, but traces of smaller game were found. The turkey has been extinct on these same meadows less than one hundred years. Fish of many kinds have been recognized from the scattered bones, jaws, with teeth and spines, and frequently the large horny plates of the sturgeon are found. It is said that these were used as knives, their edges being made sharper by grinding. It is very likely, and knives of jasper, of just such shape and size, are not uncommon. Of course, the Indian well knew the merit of our oyster, as the huge shell heaps on the sea-coast testify, but here he was content to use our river mussels, and with proper seasoning they can be made palatable. I have known one to be worried down, backed by a wad of pepper-grass. Mussel shells, like sturgeon scales, were also used as knives.

With a food supply as varied as this (and nothing whatever has been surmised), an ordinary meal or an extraordinary feast can readily be recalled, so far as its essential features are concerned. It is now September, and save where the ground has been ruthlessly uptorn, everywhere is a wealth of early autumn bloom. A soothing quiet rests upon the scene, bidding us to retrospective thought. Not a bit of stone, of pottery or a burned and blackened fragment of bone but stands out in the mellow sunshine as the feature of a long forgotten feast. A I dreamily gaze upon the gatherings of half a day, I seem to see that ancient folk that once dwelt in this neglected spot; seem to be a guest at a pre-Columbian dinner in New Jersey.

THE MUSKRAT AS
A MODERN DAINTY

Atlantic City.   Chapter XXI.

"Let's walk up to the Inlet and take a half dozen raw." A commonplace suggestion, but how interesting if you care anything about the family affairs of the oyster, especially the famous Absecon oyster of Atlantic City.

A Plate of Absecons   To begin with you may be surprised to know that the oyster is a Jersey farm product. The great area of soil which is always coming down the little rivers is the agency which makes the Absecon possible.

The most valuable part of the soil of this great tract of farming land, ultimately finds its way to the bay, in whose quiet waters it makes a long halt on its journey to the ocean, and it is deposited in the form of fine, light, black sediment, known as oyster-mud.

This is just as valuable to man, and just as fit to nourish plants as the mud which settles every year on the wheat fields and rice fields of Egypt. It is a natural fertilizer of inestimable importance, and it is so rich in organic matter that it putrefies in a few hours when exposed to the sun. In the shallow waters of the bay, under the influence of the warm sunlight, it produces a most luxuriant vegetation ; but with few exceptions, the plants which grow upon it are microscopic and invisible, and their very existence is unknown to all except a few naturalists. The oyster obtains the lime for its shell from the water, and while the amount dissolved in each gallon is very small, it extracts enough to provide for the slow growth of the shell. It is very important that the shell be built up as rapidly as possible, for the oyster has many enemies continually on the watch for thin-shelled specimens. In the lower part of the bay I have leaned over a wharf and watched the sheepshead moving up and down with their noses close to the piles,

crushing the shells
of the young oysters
between their jaws and
sucking out the soft bodies.
As I watched them I have seen
the juices from the bodies of the
little oysters streaming down from
the corners of their mouths, to be swept
away by the tide.

In order that the oyster may grow rapidly, and may be securely protected from its enemies, it must have lime. The lime in the water of the bay is derived in great part from the springs of the interior, which, flowing through limestone regions, carry some of it away in solution, and this is finally carried down the rivers and into the bay. Some of it is no doubt derived from deposits of rock in the bed of the ocean, and some from the soil along the shores, but the oyster obtains a very considerable portion of its lime in a much more direct way, by the decomposition of old oyster shells. On the oyster-beds an old shell is soon honeycombed by boring sponges and other animals, and as soon as the sea-water is thus admitted to its interior, it is rapidly dissolved and diffused. In a few years nothing is left. It has all gone back into a form which makes it available as oyster food, and it soon begins its transformation into new oyster shells. If all the shells could be returned to the beds, this source of supply would be greatly increased.

The full-grown oyster is able to live and flourish in soft mud so long as it is not buried too deeply for the open edge of the shell to reach above the mud and draw a constant supply of water to its gills; but the oyster embryo would be ingulfed and smothered at once if it were to fall on such a bottom, and in order to have the least chance of survival it must find some solid substance upon which to fasten itself, to preserve it from sinking in the soft mud, or from being buried under it as it shifts with wind and tide. In the deposits which form the soft bottom of sounds and estuaries solid bodies of any sort rarely occur, and the so-called rocks of the Chesapeake are not ledges or reefs, but accumulations of oyster shells.

The Struggle of Life

A young oyster which settles upon a natural oyster-bed has a much better chance of survival than one which settles anywhere else, and a natural bed thus tends to perpetuate itself and to persist as a definite, well-defined area. As the flood-tide rushes up the channels it stirs up the fine mud which has been deposited in the deep water. The mud is swept up on to the shallows along the shore, and if these are level, much of the sediment settles there. If, however, the flat is covered by groups of oysters, the ebbing tide does not flow off in an even sheet, but is broken up into thousands of small channels, through which the sediment flows down, to be swept out to sea. The oyster-bed thus tends to keep itself clean, and it follows that the more firmly established an oyster-bed is the better is its chance of perpetuation, since the young spat finds more favorable conditions where there are oysters, or at least shells already, than it finds anywhere else. Now, the practical importance of this description of a natural bed is this: Since it tends to remain permanent, because of the presence of oyster shells, the shelling of bottoms where there are no oysters furnishes a means for establishing new beds or for increasing the area of the old ones. The oyster dredgers state, with perfect truth, that by breaking up the crowded clusters of oysters and by scattering the shells, the use of the dredge tends to enlarge the oyster-beds. *Ancient Oyster Beds*

Although the development of this industry on a large scale is quite modern, seed oysters for planting have been raised artificially upon a small scale in Italy for more than a thousand years, by a very simple method. Pliny relates that the artificial breeding of oysters was first undertaken by a Roman knight, Sergius Orata, in the waters of Lake Avernus, and that the enterprise was so successful that its director soon became very rich. At the present day the methods which were introduced, and probably invented by Orata, are still employed by the oyster cultivators of Lake Fusaro, a small salt-water lake.

In quite modern times the study of these old methods of oyster culture has resulted in the development of the improved methods which are now employed in France. In 1853, M. De Bon, then Commissioner of Marine, was directed by the Minister to attempt to restock certain exhausted beds by planting new oysters upon them, and during this work, which was perfectly successful, he discovered that, contrary to the general opinion, the oyster can reproduce itself after it has been transplanted to bottoms on which it never before existed, and he at once commenced a series of experiments to discover some way to collect the spat emitted by those oysters, and he soon devised a successful apparatus, which consisted of a rough board floor, raised about eight inches above the bottom, near low-tide mark, covered by loose bunches of twigs.

An average Maryland oyster of good size lays about sixteen million eggs, and if half of these were to develop into female oysters, we should have from a single female eight million female descendants in the first

Some Calculations

generation, and in the second, eight million times eight million or 64,000,-000,000,000. In the third generation we would have eight million times this or 213,000,000,000.000,000,000. In the fourth, 4,096,000,000,-000,000,000,000,000,000. In the fifth, 33,600,000,000,000,000,000,-000,000,000,000,000,000 female oysters and as many males, or, in all, 66,000,000,000,000,000,000,000,000,000,000,000.

Having thus embarked upon the limitless sea of statistical fact I prepared to further enhance the appreciation of my companion for the festive and toothsome oyster, but he had fled from the scene. Some people have a strange dislike for concrete knowledge as expressed in numerals.

Atlantic City.   Chapter XVII.

There are frequent points of descent from the Boardwalk to the wide space of shore in front.

The wife and her sister and her cousin have a simultaneous craving to "come unto these yellow sands," and a little fair-complexioned niece of mine has long had, however she has smothered that longing. So *A Pen Picture of the Beach* we descend, and soon we have that pleasant sensation (a belt of dry yielding dust passed) of standing upon the firm cool sand. Hey, for the treasures of the shore ! Alice must have her shoes and socks off, and be let loose to scamper and to paddle at her will. Let her race about to her heart's content, leaving the wet sands slowly to efface the gleaming prints of her little naked feet, or let her select a firm swell of sand, and with busy spade erect an edifice, while we elders dwell again on the well-worn thought, how, indeed, this is a type of the labor of many a life ; how many spend the hours between morning and evening, just merely in sand-architecture ; then death brims up in full flood, and the shore is empty of them, and all their busy labor is levelled, and has left no mark, and is as though it had never been. For when at last the tide goes down, you shall not discover it ; it was not like a rock wall, that was submerged for a while, but appears when the waters draw off. The builder is not there : " He passed away, and lo ! he was not : yea, I sought him, but he could not be found." The builder is gone, and his works do follow him. There is nothing to show in eternity for all the long and careful labors of time.

How furrowed are the sands when the tide has drawn away from them ! There was such sparkle and glee when the pleased waters were

The Tides of Life

swelling and glittering over this tract; but they drew off by degrees, and now how all the smooth face is mapped out in furrows and wrinkles! It is tired of its toys, the fickle sea; it has left behind, little prized, these shells and seaweed, these smooth pebbles; these round chalk marbles, and pyramids and cones of spar. But it cannot rest; see it is coming back again even now; the far murmur grows into a hoarse roar; the silver curves hasten each after each along the level sand; for a time it was sick at heart, and tired of all; moaning, bankrupt, broken-hearted, weary, just now; quitting, as worthless, its possessions and its playthings; and now the turn has come; the old eagerness has awakened, the thoughtless, fervent pursuit is resumed. Ah! some do indeed make life a series of rises and fallings of the tide; now it is a loss, and they leave life's bare shore to moan in solitude far from men; now another prize has allured them, and see how earnest and continuous the plashing, ever-advancing pursuit again. Deso‑  late, bankrupt just now; but a second object attracts, and the old excitement and eagerness return. This in some cases, but not always, nor often.

O nature, quiet nature! we cannot then keep our thoughts, ourselves rather, out of you; you must ever suggest to us the sad or strange or glad realities of our own life; you are ever a parable, an allegory, of which the history of man is the ready interpretation. The song of a bird; the tint of a sunset; the dance of the falling snow; the thud of the waves advancing or retreating—these are but the accompaniment to which the life of man is the glad or sober song.

There was a time with most of us when we neither knew nor cared from what quarter the wind blew—when we had not the remotest conception

that the direction of the air-currents could concern us at all. Those were
the days of childhood's happy ignorance; when we knew nothing of the
contents of the human thorax beyond what others chose to tell us;   **A Word on**
when lungs, and liver and heart, were things we sometimes heard   **the East Wind**
mentioned, but did not trouble our heads about, having very vague notions
of their existence; when the stomach was only known by its cravings, and
the nerves were a mystery intelligible only to elderly people. A blissful
state of things that, more permanent, it would appear, among our ancestors
than with the average of mortals now-a-days. The first practical idea
about the east wind that a young fellow gets hold of is that it is good for
sliding and skating, because it locks up the canals and streams, and covers
the ponds and ornamental waters with practicable ice. We can well recall
the eagerness and the profound interest with which we used to watch the
weathercock on the church tower in our skating days, and the mortification,
not to say disgust, with which we saw the brazen indicator veer spitefully
southwards.

As we grow older we grow more conscious of the mysterious ma-
chinery within us, and the atmospheric conditions without us, and of the
marvellous and ominous sympathy there is between the two. But if we
are in average health it is long before we begin to quarrel with the east
wind. For a time we love to face it, and even take it to our embrace,
feeling that it is a mighty breath, strong to build up the stalwart frame and
renew the energies of youth. We revel in it, and, rejoicing in the freshness
it brings, and the vigor it imparts, can repeat with pleasure Mr. Kingsley's
A Boisterous   rhapsody in praise of the east wind.
Friend   But by-and-by we find it rather too much for us—just a *leetle* too
boisterous and rude; and though we hardly confess to that much, we catch
ourselves shirking its proffered embrace, shunting ourselves to the lee side
of available shelter when it blows hard, and buttoning up to the chin when
it must needs be encountered. Still, we *can* encounter it, and get the better

of it too, in a brisk walk or a gay canter along the open downs; and we do so occasionally, perhaps pluming ourselves on our hardiness. But it may happen that we do it once too often, or without sufficient care, and then the east wind gets a grip of our breathing apparatus, and shows that he is master by consigning us to the bed or the easy chair, to a slop diet and teetotalism—to the hot mustard "foots." When a man, verging, say upon the fifth age of Shakespeare, has had one or two experiences of this kind, it is truly marvellous to note how learned he becomes upon the subject of the east

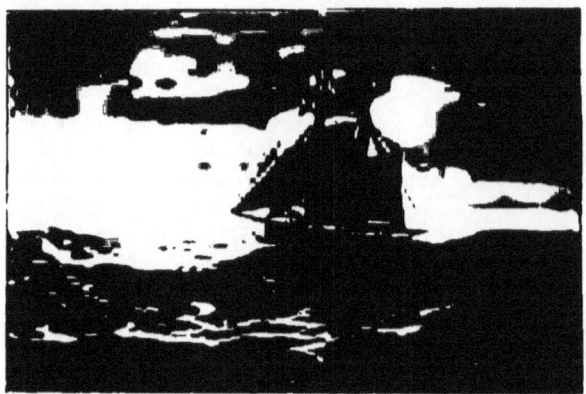

wind. He need not look at the weathercock for information; he has an index with him—a sort of weather-gauge—that tells him when it is coming, as sure as a gun; he scents it afar, even while sitting by his fireside; can tell of its advent twenty, thirty, forty hours before its arrival; he will wake up in the night and say to his wife, "The wind is getting into the east," and, turning under the blankets, go to sleep again to dream of it and the plagues it may bring with it. He does not indorse the poet's invocation—

"Hail to thee, north-easter!"

—rather he dreads its approach and only hopes to have done with it as soon as possible.

The east wind caroms upon Atlantic City at an acute angle, and although it may come to us laden with the fogs of Newfoundland its effects are felt less than at any other place upon the coast.

Nothing else so strongly appeals to the imagination of the frequenter of the sea-coast as the mysteries of its myriad victims—the countless ships which are scattered upon its sunless floor, gone from the ken of man and forgotten in the limbo of time past and blotted from memory.

The Floor of the Sea

The idea that ships are likely to be buried in the accumulations which are forming on the deeper sea-floor, rests upon a mistaken conception as to the speed with which sediments are laid down at a distance from the shore. These deposits of the open oceans are so slowly made that we must decree it excessive to suppose that a depth of a single inch can be formed in a thousand years. It is likely that in no case, save near the coast-line, or in the rare places where the showers of volcanic waste bring an unusually large amount of detritus, can a ship be buried in the accumulating strata so as to be preserved in a recognizable form. If the creatures of the far future, to whom it may be given to scan the rocks which are now forming and are hereafter to be uplifted into dry land, are to find a trace of their remote ancestors in the deposits, they will secure it not by finding the hulks of great vessels, probably not from the bones of men or the common implements which serve them in seafaring, but from the objects composed of glass, or more likely those made of the rarer metals, such as gold and platinum. Of the vast wreckage of an iron warship such as the Captain, which sank in the Bay of Biscay, the hulk, great guns, shot and shell, the timber, and all the forms of its crew will probably disappear before they are entombed in the slowly gathered strata. The geological remainder will perhaps be the coal of her fuel store, the gold of the watches and trinkets and the massive glass objects which abound in such a ship; in all but a

171

small and little indicative part of what went to the bottom of the sea when the vessel foundered. It has, to many persons, been an interesting speculation as to the aspect of the countless wrecks which have been swallowed up by the North Atlantic since the churn of waters has been ploughed by the keels of ships. Their number is probably to be reckoned by the tens of thousands, and the greater part of them lie in a comparatively small part of that field. If we count this portion of the Atlantic which is most peopled with wrecks as having an area of 3,000,000 square miles, and estimate the total number of such ruins within this space as 30,000, we would have an average of one sunken ship for each hundred square miles of surface.

A BALTIMORE BELLE AND TWO PHILADELPHIANS

Atlantic City.   Chapter XXIII.

[Angus Sinclair, in *Locomotive Engineering* for August, 1898:]

"It has been my privilege to ride on a great many fast trains in America and Great Britain. I have a habit of carrying a stop watch and of using it to time the speed between mile posts, which practice has given me positive evidence of the speed attained or maintained. **The Fastest Train**

After watching the speed of celebrated trains in the British Isles, I have at certain times been moved to remark to railway men and others that some trains in America made better time than those of other countries. When I proceeded, by referring to my note book, to give particulars, the best of friends would regard me with a pitying smile which said as plainly as possible 'he has acquired skill in the Yankee habit of boasting and lying.'

A Run to the Shore   As I am going to be visiting among railway friends abroad for a few weeks I wished to witness for myself the run of the fastest train in the world, that runs from Camden to Atlantic City, a distance of 55.5 miles in 50 minutes, an average speed of 62.2 miles per hour. Through the courtesy of Mr. Theodore Voorhees, Vice-President of the Philadelphia and Reading Railway, I received permission to ride on the engine of that celebrated train. The train is due to leave Camden, which is across the Delaware River from Philadelphia, at 3.50 P. M., and I was there in good time to witness the preliminary touches given to the locomotive before starting upon a trip that must put a severe test upon various elements of the engine.

Half an hour before starting time the engine was backed up to the train, which consisted of seven passenger cars. I happened to be

NEW FERRY HOUSE OF THE ATLANTIC CITY RAILROAD
PHILADELPHIA & READING RAILWAY

exceptionally fortunate to take notes of an extraordinary feat of fast train running, for it was the first time that seven cars had been hauled on this train, five or six cars having been the usual load last season. Each car averages 75,000 pounds, and the engine, in working order with tender, weighs about 218,000 pounds, so there were 525,000 pounds of train, making a total of 743,000 pounds, or 371½ tons to be moved. *The Big Engine*

I found a crowd of interested admirers about the engine watching every move of the engineer and fireman, both of whom were quietly attending to the duties of preparing the engine to do its work without chance of failure. The engineer, Mr. Charles H. Fahl, kept moving about the engine scanning every part, and dropping a little oil on the parts that needed the greatest amount of lubrication. While I remained watching him he oiled the principal bearings twice, and then carried his cans to the cab, apparently satisfied that his full duty had been performed. The fireman, Mr. John Pettit, was engaged throwing a few shovelfuls of coal at brief intervals into the enormous firebox which has 86 square feet of grate area, and watching at intervals to find a thin spot that needed covering up.

These trains were run for three months last year on the 50 minute schedule, with the same men on the engine, without a single mishap, or without losing a minute of time. The engine never had a hot pin or bearing, and, in spite of the tremendous work put upon it, was always ready to turn round and take out another train without a minute's delay. That fine record was due to the care in seeing that everything was in good order before the start was made. In conversing with Vice-President Voorhees I found that he attributed the successful running of this train in a great measure to the care and skill of the engineer and fireman.

The Start At 3.50 precisely the signal came to start and the engine moved ahead without slip or quiver. A few turns of the great driving wheels forced the train into good speed and away we rushed out through the yards, through the suburban residences and away past smiling vegetable larms. On reaching the first mile post to be seen, which was about a mile out, I had my watch in hand and the second one was passed in 68 seconds. An interval of 62 seconds brought us to the following post, and then the succeeding notations were 60, 59, 56, 52, 50, 48, 46, 52, 53, 53, 51, 50, 52, 49, 50, 53, 52, 50, 49, 44, 45, 42, 44 seconds for each succeeding mile. Then I made up my mind that the high speed was authentic and put my watch in my pocket the better to note particulars about the handling of the engine.

In the Cab I was sitting on the fireman's side and could not see how the engineer was handling his reverse lever and throttle lever, but I noticed that there was no change in the point of cut off after the train was going forty miles an hour, and it seemed to me that the steam was permitted to follow the piston at a little more than half stroke. The steam pressure gauge could be easily noted, and the safety valve blew off at 230 pounds per gauge pressure. The fireman appeared to do his best to keep the pressure about five pounds short of the popping point, and he did his work well, but the indications were that he had more difficulty in keeping the steam down to the popping point than in letting it rise. He did not seem to work much on the fire. He watched it very closely, and threw in a few lumps occasionally, but there was no hard work in supplying all the steam needed to do the enormous work of pulling the heavy train at the speed noted. The coal used was small lump similar to house furnace coal.

The road is a little undulating, but the rises and descends seemed to make little difference to the speed. Out through stretches of farm lands, away through spreading woods and moor-like regions of scrub oaks the train rushed along, neither curve nor grade seeming to restrain its velocity. The engine rode with astonishing smoothness. When I have ridden on other engines working hard and keeping up speed over 70 miles an hour, there was always a harsh vertical vibration due probably to the jerk of compression, but that disagreeable sensation was entirely absent in this compound. The work done gauged in horse power per hour was enormous, and perhaps unprecedented for a locomotive, but it was performed with remarkable smoothness, and the impression was always present that the engine still had some margin of power in reserve which could be used if necessary.

About four miles from Atlantic City a signal was against the train and the speed was reduced to about 20 miles an hour before the signal was

PHILA. & READING RAILWAY LOCOMOTIVE USED FOR FAST SERVICE ON THE ATLANTIC CITY RAILROAD

lowered. That was about three-quarters of a mile from the succeeding mile post. I noted the time from that mile post to the next one and the mile was run in 60 seconds. That will give a good idea of the power of the engine.   *Over 70 Miles an Hour*

Two minutes were used in running the last two miles through the switches. At least one minute was lost with the signal check. With these deductions I calculate that the average run was made at a speed of over 70 miles an hour."

Atlantic City. Chapter XXIV.

[Extracts from an article which appeared in the *Century Magazine*, for January, 1898, which very aptly portrays Atlantic City of to-day and furnishes ample demonstration and proof for the now practically undisputed title of "the greatest all the year resort of the world:"]

Atlantic City as a Winter and Spring Resort

"During the winter, according to the reports issued by the weather bureau, the thermometer at Atlantic City averages higher than at any other point on the North Atlantic Coast. The fact needs no proof, for it is evident almost at once to any visitor. But the explanation requires some observation of the course of the Gulf Stream. This great river of warm water approaches so near to the coast of New Jersey that it furnishes an excellent natural "hot-water" system for warming the sea-breezes that constantly sweep over this great city of the coast.

The Gulf Stream

One may say with little exaggeration that the waves which wash the Florida Coast are the same as those that here visit the Northern States. At no other point does the great Stream make a "P. P. C." call before setting out upon its voyage across the ocean to look after the comfort of our British Cousins. Fortunately the comparative warmth of the climate during the winter is not followed by the same rise of temperature in the summer. Owing to the nearness of the great Ocean, which acts as a

regulator of heat, Atlantic City is emphatically a resort for all the year. Cooled by sea-breezes in summer, and, strange as it may seem, warmed by the same breezes during the winter, the result is an equal climate that is

The Music of the Surf   exactly adapted for those enjoying good health or for invalids. The thunder of the sea along the shore is heard at once upon alighting from the train ; and it is but a few minutes' ride to any of the many delightful hotels that the throng of visitors has caused to spring up all along the wonderful beach. Ordinarily, the journey to a warmer climate is so long and tedious that it serves to discourage the visits of those who are in good health, even if it does not make it impossible for invalids to secure a needed change of climate. Then, too, no one wishes unnecessarily to put himself out of reaching distance of his own home and friends. It is sometimes most essential that a return should be possible at almost a moment's notice, and where one is seeking health, to go into a distant land, or to make a journey of hundreds of miles, might neutralize any possible benefits expected from the trip.

    Proverbially ignorant of the advantages of their own country, few Americans know that Atlantic City is the largest, richest, most popular, and, in short, the finest watering place in the world. Its "season" never comes to an end, which alone gives it a great advantage over all resorts of the kind, for the proprietors of its hotels need not reckon upon making the profits of one season carry them over a dull time. There are forty millions of dollars' worth of property within the city limits, as estimated by the State Comptroller, and not a little of this value is due to the many miles of seaside homes owned by the well-to-do and fashionable of the world, who have discovered here advantages lacking elsewhere. As a result, houses are magnificent and the avenues are broad, clean and well-kept, the owners showing a spirit of rivalry in making houses as attractive as possible. The location being so favorable, and the climate so exceptional, the railroad facilities are of the best, and the hotels are in the hands of most enterprising owners. The fastest regular trains in the world, according to the *Scientific American*, are those running between Atlantic City and Philadelphia. These lines, of course, connect this resort closely with all parts of the country.

A Pen Picture As for the beach itself, everything possible has been done to make it attractive. The "Esplanade" or ocean steel walk is the name given to a walk five miles long and forty feet wide that is parallel to the edge of the ocean. It used to be called the Boardwalk, but since it has all been rebuilt the name is not quite appropriate, for it rests on a framework of steel, and is as secure as an iron pier throughout its whole extent. Along the line of the shore there is nothing to cut off a view of Old Ocean except an occasional pavilion in which are comfortable seats where promenaders can rest. The walk itself is from six to twelve feet above the sand, and is guarded by a metal railing on the side toward the ocean, while along the shore side will be found shops, bathing houses, and booths for the sale of whatever can attract visitors. When it is said that a quarter of a million dollars have been spent in making this walk all that it should be, it will be understood that the steel walk is something more than a line of planks with which other seashore resorts are occasionally provided. In winter and summer the walk is thronged with pleasure seekers or those who have come here for health and rest. Shakespeare's "Seven Ages" each finds thousands of representatives. Here one may see the red-cheeked, bright eyed school-girl, swinging breezily along, enjoying the enfranchisement which the new time has brought to her; the matron who, tired by the turmoil of the town, finds rest in the tumult of the sea, while about her are children, unconsciously

CAUGHT BY THE LENS

breathing in health, though thinking only of pleasure; professional and business men renewing their youth far from the counting-room and the court; the philosopher and the idler, side by side, sunning themselves in the salt air, forgetting that there is to life any side but this.

As mildly temperate breezes turn winter into summer, so electricity turns night into day along this crowded thoroughfare. Truly, the throng does not seem to diminish at night. The old lady from the country who asked, upon first seeing the crowd upon Broadway, "What church is out?" might be excused for inquiring, as she gazed upon the thronged esplanade, where all these people find lodgment. But when she had learned how many hotels Atlantic City supports, her wonder would be whence came all the people who fill them. It is claimed that no other city has a greater number of hotels and boarding-houses and the claim will be conceded at first glance. Indeed, it may be said that every building which is not either a hotel or a boarding house is a private cottage for the accommodation of visitors from the cities. One hundred and seventy-five thousand people can be cared for within Atlantic City, and besides those who go and come, there is a permanent population of twenty-five thousand. With such a number of inhabitants, it is hardly necessary to say that Atlantic City is a municipality perfectly equipped in all respects, and prides itself upon the enterprise and energy with which its affairs are conducted. There is a perfect sewerage system, a trolley line eight miles long, traversing the beach, well-paved streets, electric lights, and—most important of all—an ample water supply from artesian wells and springs, besides first class fire and police departments. The only complaint that can be made in regard to the police department is that its excellently disciplined force has not enough to do.

A Round of Pleasure

The old principle of "supply and demand" explains the excellent equipment of this seaport resort, for the people who gather here are used to the luxuries and delicacies of life, and familiar with the dainty

surroundings offered them by the capitals of the world. Naturally there is a numerous leisure class of the best type, and outdoor sports flourish, while theatres, dances, card parties and other entertainments never cease in the many hotels.

In the winter and spring, New York, Boston, Philadelphia and Baltimore send thousands of representatives to this city by the sea, and perhaps from February until June the island is at its best. The villas are filled with gay house parties, and the hotel-registers show the names of guests distinguished in the professional, political, or social world.

One advantage of this favored child of the Gulf Stream has not yet been mentioned. Although surrounded by salt water, the air of the island is exceptionally dry, and physicians agree that its climate is the most pleasant and invigorating in the world. Under the supervision of the best medical talent, with the aid of hot and cold sea-water baths and her ozone-laden air, her dry, crisp breezes from pine forests, and her wealth of sunshine, Atlantic City performs marvelous cures. *For Invalids*

Not the least of the advantages offered to the invalid is that of being surrounded by the strong and healthy sportsmen, who come, with guns and rods, to enjoy the best hunting and fishing to be found along the coast. Who does not know the reputation of the great game beaches of Brigantine and Barnegat? Who has not heard of the safe, speedy and comfortable fleet of fishing boats and other craft of the Atlantic City squadron? The succession of game and fowl, each in its season, is varied and attractive. Snipe, plover, marlin, willet, yellow legs, black duck, mallard and teal flock here, as if, in spite of the eager sportsmen, they were determined to enjoy the delights of the climate. The brother of the rod and line will find schools of bluefish, sheepshead, drum, croker, codfish, herring, mackerel, sea-bass and weakfish.

When it is understood that Atlantic City has every convenience of comfort and luxury to be found in great cities, it will be seen that it is impossible to do more than refer to the many-sided attractions here collected. The schools, both public and private, are excellent. There are churches of every denomination, and several well known charitable institutions, such as the Children's Seashore Home, the Mercer Memorial Home and the City Hospital.

Schools, Churches and Charities

One can sum up by saying that Atlantic City possesses in perfection every attribute that one could expect in a seashore resort, and enjoys exceptional repute among the medical profession as a home for invalids in need of wholesome rest and the tonic of the sea air. It may fairly lay claim to the title, "Queen of American Watering Places."

Atlantic City. Chapter XXV.

The steel tentacles of the Pennsylvania Railroad are spread across New Jersey, touching the seashore at Long Branch, and by means of its line between that point and Barnegat Pier it touches the score of beautiful and popular intermediate resorts, including Asbury Park, Belmar, Spring Lake, Sea Girt, Point Pleasant, Bay Head, Mantoloking, Lavalette, Ortley, Berkeley and Seaside Park. It also extends a branch to all points upon Long Beach. It operates two routes to Atlantic City with spurs which reach Somers' Point and Longport, with an admirable ferry service between these places.

Penna. R. R. Routes to the Coast

The West Jersey Division extends to Ocean City, Sea Isle City, Avalon, Stone Harbor, Anglesea, Wildwood, Holly Beach and Cape May. The rails of this line also touch Delaware Bay at Salem and Maurice River.

In handling the enormous traffic to and from Atlantic City its trains are run both from Broad Street Station direct and via the splendid new ferry station at the foot of Market Street. The trains from the Broad Street Terminal start westward, describing a great semicircle through the upper section of Philadelphia and cross a magnificent bridge which spans the Delaware River above the city.

The old Camden & Atlantic Railroad, the detailed history of which is fully related upon earlier pages, is now the Pennsylvania's direct passenger route to Atlantic City. The entire roadway has been rebuilt and double-tracked with standard steel rails.

To one who recalls the discomforts and vicissitudes of a railroad journey in the early days between Camden and Atlantic City, the swift,

NEW FERRY HOUSE AND STATION OF THE PENNSYLVANIA RAILROAD AT THE FOOT OF MARKET STREET, PHILADELPHIA

clean run of the present seems to fully express the progress which has been made in everything relating to seashore travel.

Pretty suburban settlements are growing up all along the Pennsylvania's route as a result of the improvements in service in recent years.

The handsome ferry building recently completed by the Pennsylvania Railroad Company at the foot of Market Street, Philadelphia, is an ornament to the city. Provision is made in the design for the use of double decked ferry-boats in the future, and it is probable that in the course of time elevated trackage will extend to the limits of Camden, thus enabling engineers to make high speed from the instant of starting. 746 miles or about nine per cent. of the tracks of the Pennsylvania Railroad are in the State of New Jersey. With the single exception of the line between Trenton and New York, the Atlantic City Division is the most important.

The equipment, speed and attention to the comfort of passengers upon the seashore trains are the same as exist upon the main line, and these features are unsurpassed upon any of the great railroads of the world.

SAND
PILES

Atlantic City.   Chapter XXVI.

This new and influential organization was formed as the result of a meeting held at the Windsor Hotel, Atlantic City, in April of the present year (1899), Mr. G. Jason Waters, with whom the movement originated, being elected president. The purpose is to maintain an annual horse show which will attract leading horse owners and the many interested in fine animals and equipages to this resort upon such occasions.

Atlantic City Horse Show Association

The first of these exhibits was held July 13, 14 and 15 at the Inlet Park and proved an unqualified success. The exhibits included roadsters, hackneys, horses in harness, saddle horses, polo ponies, hunters and jumpers, four-in-hands, fire horses and apparatus, hotel coaches, delivery wagons, baggage wagons, etc.

The Club is composed of the following gentlemen:— G. Jason Waters, President; Charles Evans, Vice-President; Hon. Allen B. Endicott, Treasurer; Walter J. Buzby, Secretary; William S. Blitz, Assistant Secretary. Directors: G. Jason Waters, Hon. Joseph Thompson, Walter J. Buzby, F. W. Hemsley, J. H. Lippincott, H. W. Leeds, D. S. White, Jr., Edward S. Lee, A. O. Dayton, A. C. McClellan, Dr. J. R. Fleming, Jacob Myers, W. H. Catlin, A. J. Nutting, Morton W. Smith, Charles Evans, Hon. Allen B. Endicott, J. D. Southwick, Philip J. Leigh, Josiah White, J. H. Borton, Newlin Haines, W. E. Edge, Charles R. Myers, J. B. Reilly, Dr. M. D. Youngman, Charles Lackey, John G. Shreve, John M. Shaw. Executive Committee: G. Jason Waters, Hon. Allen B. Endicott, Charles Evans, Edward S. Lee.

Atlantic City. Chapter XXVIII.

[Extract from article in *Therapeutic Gazette*, February 15, 1898, by William Edgar Darnall, A. B., M. D.:]

Distinguished Testimony Forty years ago, when the beautiful island on which Atlantic City is built was an arid waste of sand, Philadelphia physicians recognized the wonderful health-giving properties of the climate it possesses. At first an occasional patient courageously ventured to the place; later, as hotels went up, they came in greater numbers; at the present day the wide-spread fame of this resort draws health seekers from all parts of the world. Abundant evidence from most credible sources now exists as to its usefulness in many forms of disease. It will be my purpose in this paper to describe some of the local conditions and causes that contribute to this remarkable climate.

From meteorological tables, geographical and other data, a general opinion can be formed as to the nature of the climate of a section and whether it is favorable or unfavorable to health. It will generally be found, however, that there are strictly local conditions which should enter into consideration in determining whether a given locality is or is not the best place to send a case. **The Climate of Atlantic City and its Usefulness in Disease**

"Climate is so dependent upon purely local conditions, pertaining often to only a limited area of territory, that it is impossible for any work based solely upon official data taken at fixed points to convey anything more than a generalization. These conditions can only be ascertained by a careful study of the localities claiming the patronage of the health seeker. The physician who prescribes climatic change for his patient on

A MISUNDER-
STANDING

generalizations will benefit just about as large a proportion of them as if he filled his prescriptions for all his patients from the same bottle. The ideal health resort must have natural conditions on which to build."*

Geographically Atlantic City is situated on an island just off the coast of New Jersey, lying in latitude 39° 22'. This island, about three-quarters of a mile in width and ten miles in length, is completely surrounded by salt water—a point to be borne in mind. From its magnificent stretch of ocean-swept beach, an arm of water known as "The Thoroughfare" is sent around it, dividing it from the mainland. Beyond this, extending shoreward, there is a five-mile expanse of salt meadow land.

The coast of New Jersey has a general direction from southwest to northeast, but the beach front of the island trends more to the west, thus causing it to face almost to the south. It is possible that this may be one of the factors accounting for some of the characteristics of its climate which are not possessed even by other Jersey resorts.

The soil is porous and sandy. Water therefore soon soaks through it, leaving no standing pools. Even the natural atmospheric moisture seems to be absorbed by the dry sand. The growth on such a soil is necessarily scant, preventing the possibility of disease which lurks in decayed vegetation.   A Mistaken Idea

It seems to be a common impression that the air at the seacoast, especially during the winter months, must necessarily be heavy and damp. This is not so by any means. One of the most distinctive features of the climate of Atlantic City is the dryness and bracing quality of the

---

* This paragraph by Dr. A. F. McKay (*Medical Record*, Oct. 31, 1897) is so much to the point that I have quoted it bodily.

atmosphere. There are of course occasional mists and foggy days; but by far the greater part of the time the air is dry, producing a feeling of buoyancy, as if it were wafted from mountain heights.

The dryness of the climate is, however, best shown by an examination of the rainfall. This will average about two and a half inches per month, or thirty inches annually. These figures are in striking contrast to those of other points along the coast. At none of them does the rainfall approach so low a point, and at many it will be seen that the annual precipitation is from 50 to 60 inches.

The question of temperature is always an important one in the study of any climate. It has gotten to be a saying among weather observers that Atlantic City breaks all rules of meteorological calculation in this regard. Severe extremes of temperature are unknown here. Even in the coldest winter weather the middle of the day is usually pleasant, the temperature at noon rarely being below 40°. As this is the most convenient time for invalids to be out, it is fortunate that it is rarely cold enough to be disagreeable to them. On the coldest day of last winter (January 27, 1897) Atlantic City showed the highest temperature of any Eastern city, and the same average temperature for the day as New Orleans. On the other hand, during the most intense heat of July and August the thermometer seldom registered above 85°, while the average temperature this time of the year is 71.5°.

The records show a mean maximum temperature for three years of 57.7°, a mean minimum of only 45.5°, or an average annual temperature of 51.6°. A daily comparison will show that it is six to ten degrees warmer here in winter than in Philadelphia, and that much cooler in summer. Comparison of Temperature There are several factors to be mentioned in accounting for this remarkable record, most important of which are: the winds; the geographical position of Atlantic City, which has been described; and the Gulf Stream. During the winter months the prevailing direction of the winds is from the west and north-west. These winds come to us across sixty miles of the sandy soil of New Jersey. They are not only warmed by the radiation of heat from it, but the sand absorbs their moisture and dries them. If the winds, on the other hand, are from the south, south-east, or east, they become heated as they pass over some three hundred miles of Gulf Stream. This leaves the north-easters as the only disagreeable winds we have. Blowing down between the Gulf Stream and the coast they have no modifying influence. These, however, are of rare occurrence, and do not last longer than a day or two at a time.

The nearness of such a large body of ocean water is itself an important agent in the modification of the climate. Sea water possesses a fairly constant temperature, which does not fluctuate much from winter to summer.

During the rigors of winter, when the earth and air are colder than the water, which remains constant, this fact causes the water to serve as a blanket by which the heat that would be lost from the soil by radiation is retained. Temperature is thus elevated in winter. In summer, however, the opposite effect is produced, for the atmosphere is now warmer than the water, and when everything is roasting inland the temperature is made refreshingly cool here by reason of the evaporation from the surface of so large a body of water, and the breezes wafted from it. In this way the climate is made more equable, and less subject to extreme or sudden changes of temperature either in winter or summer.

Days Bright and Sunny In the consideration of a place to which patients may be referred for their health, it is highly necessary that a locality be chosen which has a majority of its days bright and sunny. Dark days depress the invalid and deprive him of the sun, besides shutting him in the house, so that he also loses the benefit derived from outdoor exercise. A casual reference to statistics disproves the common impression that life by the sea must be bleak and dreary. It is safe to say that there are at least 265 days in the year on which an invalid could be out enjoying the delights of the famous Boardwalk. This leaves but 27.5 per cent. of the days—a little more than one-fourth—on which the sun hides his face entirely. Quite a percentage of these occur in March, the disagreeable month everywhere, and such weather is usually of very short duration. Most of the time the weather is bright and sunny, the air bracing and exhilarating, and the winds tempered with a softness that is surprising; while during the autumn no wealth of words can paint the glory of the sea and climate.

A JUNE MORNING

Undoubtedly the most important modifier of the climate of the Atlantic States is the influence of the Gulf Stream, which bears a peculiar relation to the coast opposite Atlantic City. It has been determined by the United States Geodetic Survey that there is a mutual relation between the moisture, temperature and barometric pressure on land and the varying velocities and different positions of the currents of the Gulf Stream. The surface velocity, according to Pilsbury, is sensibly affected by barometric differences, forming low and high areas of pressure. These currents have also daily, monthly and yearly variations in position, and each motion is no doubt governed by laws that are as yet but dimly understood. The Gulf

Stream follows the declination of the moon like a needle does a magnet. Its axis moves from west to east as the moon proceeds from high declination to low, and crosses the equator. Its volume expands and contracts. Even its temperature, which is about 80°, presents variations within narrow limits.

The conclusions adopted by Professor Bache from the observations taken under his direction were as follows: "That between Cape Florida and New York the Gulf Stream is divided into several bands of higher and lower temperature, of which the axis (of the stream) is the warmest, the temperature falling rapidly inshore and more slowly outside. This is not only the case at the surface, but with modifications easily understood at considerable depths. That between the coast and the stream there is a fall in temperature so abrupt that it has been aptly called the *cold wall*. The cold wall extends with varying dimensions and changes of its peculiar features along the coast from Cape Florida, northward as far as examined. Inside this wall of colder temperature there is another increase, while outside the warmest band, which is next the cold wall, there is another warm and one other cold band."

The innermost of these warm bands approaches as near as sixty-five miles from the coast, opposite Atlantic City. Not only its proximity to us here must be noticed, but also its course. At this point it takes a bend running a little more than a half degree of latitude to the north-east, then bending due east in latitude 40°. A certain outlying portion of Gulf Stream water, therefore, setting in the direction of this current will, when it makes this sudden turn, continue the original direction of the current, being deflected as a tangent from the curve of the stream. The beach of Atlantic City with its southern exposure is situated just where it would receive with open embrace whatever modifying influences might be derived from such a current setting in this direction. What leads me to believe this fact has some bearing on the question is that no other seaside resort even along the Jersey coast possesses exactly the climate we have here.

Formation of the Gulf Stream   It may be of some interest to digress here a little in order to describe briefly the two generally accepted scientific theories of the causes of the formation of this remarkable body of water known as the Gulf Stream. These are the (*a*) Wind Theory and the (*b*) Density Theory.

(*a*) The *Wind Theory*, of which Pilsbury is an advocate, supposes that any permanent wind blowing constantly in the same direction across a body of water will cause such friction between the surface particles and the lower strata of the air that these particles will tend to move with the wind; also the wind caught behind the crests of waves would push these along. The friction thus produced among the surface particles of water is transmitted from layer to layer, with continually diminishing force as the depth increases. It was calculated by Agassiz that 100,000 years was ample time to allow friction of this sort to be communicated from the surface to the bottom—a depth say, of 2000 fathoms. It is held therefore that the trade winds blowing in the same direction for ages, over the Atlantic Ocean, have by this friction process, slow in itself yet attaining a mighty momentum as the centuries have rolled on, been able to move this vast body of water along in a constant stream.

(*b*) The advocates of the *Density Theory* hold that ocean currents owe their origin to the difference between the specific gravity of sea water at one place and sea water at another place; whether this be due to difference of saltness, temperature or what-not, it disturbs equilibrium so that currents result.

The effect of heat, as at the equator, causes a lesser density of the surface water, while the effect of the cold of the polar regions causes a greater density. This latter being heavier sinks as it is cooled by reason of its greater specific gravity and diminishing bulk, and sinking, causes a flow of water to be drawn into its basin from the surrounding surface area of water. Such a supply must come from a yet greater distance ; and so this cooling causes a set of water in the direction of the poles, when a corresponding deep-down current of cold water sets toward the equator to be again heated.

Evaporation and Precipitation

Also precipitation over the central portion of the water hemisphere of the earth is greatly in excess of evaporation. Northwards evaporation is in excess of precipitation. The water thus drawn from polar seas by evaporation is quickly hurried down to the areas of low barometric pressure, where precipitation follows. But its loss from the polar regions makes the basin referred to above still larger, and so adds an additional impetus to the set of the water northward. The disturbance of equilibrium thus produced between equatorial and polar water, by cooling and evaporation, causes a steady current to flow from gulf to poles, and a return undercurrent from poles to the equator.

These are in brief the two most prominent among the many theories that have been advanced as to the formation of the Gulf Stream. It must be true that warm water comes from the equator and cold from the polar regions, and whatever be the mode of transfer the modification of climate is due to its presence rather than to the method of its delivery.

But to return to Atlantic City. After having studied the meteorological conditions and geographical environments that conduce to its unique climate, the practical question naturally arises, What is it good for ? What classes of disease will receive benefit by a sojourn in such a climate ? Climatology is a subject beset with many and peculiar difficulties. While a great and growing department of therapy, it is as yet but dimly understood by the bulk of the profession. Formerly climatic change was only thought of as a remedial agent in respiratory diseases. Now every chronic deviation from health is studied with reference to change. Such change, however, must not be recommended in a haphazard way. There must be some rational basis underlying it if any good is to be derived therefrom. **Tonic and Alterative Climate**

The climate of Atlantic City is a dry one, tonic and alterative in its qualities. Its air is both a stimulant and a sedative. Actual experience drawn from many sources has demonstrated that those suffering from almost all functional disturbances, nervous prostration, overwork of both mind and body, depression from any cause, indigestion, insomnia, or any torpid state of the system, as well as strumous conditions and diatheses, are much benefited by the bracing qualities of the air. Residence here has proven of inestimable value to that elderly class of cases whose health and strength seem to have forsaken them, making them chronic invalids. Long-lasting and obstinate diseases of women rebellious to treatment at home oftentimes show marked improvement or disappear entirely under the alterative influence of the air here.

There is a class of cases in the practice of nearly every physician whose management becomes very trying to his skill. These are the convalescents from severe and exhausting diseases or operations who seem to reach a standstill. They remain without improvement of vitality or appetite till the patience of the family becomes exhausted, while the physician pursues resources clear to the end of his string without avail. Such cases usually have an appetite before they have been here twenty-four hours; they seem to improve almost as they cross the meadows. As soon as they come under the influence of the stimulating air oxidation is increased. Its soporific effect is at the same time a sedative to a disordered nervous system. Its purity and freedom from unsanitary conditions and miasmatic influences allows more rapid elimination of deleterious matter from the system.

On the other hand, the softness of the air and its balmy warmth soothes the stiffened joints of the gouty and rheumatic; relieves the distress of emphysema and asthma, especially those cases coming from inland or from high altitudes. There are some asthmatics, however, whose difficulties are aggravated by coming here. These should seek the warmer, more sedative climate of the far South. The cases that do not do well at the seashore will oftentimes be relieved by the mountains, and *vice versa*.

Immunity from Hay Fever Whether due to the antiseptic and alterative qualities of the atmosphere, or to the absence of the pollen of vegetation, sufferers from hay-fever enjoy comparative immunity from their malady. Atlantic City has been referred to as a "hay-fever paradise!" Most noteworthy perhaps and most striking is the number of people living here who have been cured of chronic bronchial and catarrhal affections. This is no doubt brought about by the alterative influence of iodine, bromine, chlorine, oxygen, and the ammonia salts, with which every inspiration they breathe is laden. At the same time it must be remembered that the air is pure and free from the dust of a city, factory smoke, exhalations from slum districts, and other impurities that serve to keep up an irritation once started in the respiratory tract.

Skin diseases are not common here. They are often mitigated or disappear entirely, for the atmosphere, while dry, is not irritating to the skin like that of high climates.

The profession formerly held that high altitudes were better adapted to beginning cases of phthisis. The trend of opinion, however, now seems to be that neither wind, humidity nor altitude in themselves and apart from other factors play so important a part as do the purity of the air, its percentage of free ozone, and the absence of unsanitary conditions. Cold, humid winds chill the surface of the skin by conducting away its heat, and drive the blood inward. It is easy to see that this does an already inflamed lung no good. Such weather should always be avoided therefore by a consumptive. Raw or penetrating days will occur at times in every climate. Atlantic City, however, has a very small percentage of such days, and they soon give way to sunny weather again.

Much may be said in favor of this place as a resort for tubercular patients. Not a small advantage is its proximity to the large centers of population. Long journeys from home are always depressing to invalids. The best results may often be obtained by sending the sick one to a place near enough to his home for him to enjoy the comfort of friends, and where the change will not be too radical.

The following points have been enumerated as reasons why the well known climates of New Mexico and Southern California are model ones for phthisis, viz.: (1) a dry aseptic atmosphere; (2) a maximum of sunshine and a minimum of cloud; (3) a slight variation of temperature between extremes of heat and cold; (4) a minimum likelihood of sudden changes of temperature; (5) a light, porous soil.

A REST ON SANTA FE

If what has been said in this climatic study has been carefully followed it will be easily seen that Atlantic City meets these requirements adequately in each case, and her climate stands as the peer of any resort for phthisical patients. In the earlier stages of the disease, when it is threatening rather than in actual progress, or if the area of diseased tissue is small, not progressive, no wasting nor hectic of importance, and digestion is good, it may be recommended with confidence. This climate is especially good where tuberculosis has resulted as a part of a general breakdown from overwork, and where excavation is not rapidly extending. Cases of fibroid phthisis, or phthisis associated with catarrhal or laryngeal trouble, much nervous irritability, emphysema, bronchitis, bronchiectasis, organic heart disease, or any brain or spinal affection, and in other conditions where high altitude is directly contraindicated, will usually receive much benefit here. Even in advanced cases with double cavities, degenerative diseases of the blood vessels, ulceration of the intestines or albuminuria, temporary improvement may often take place. It is only temporary, however. The death warrant of such patients has already been written. Their best place is home, where their latter days may be made comfortable and their end be among friends. If they insist on climatic change the warm and sunny South is better for them and may prolong their lives a short time. The air here is too stimulating for this class of cases.

Biographical Sketches

of Prominent Citizens
who have helped to make
Atlantic City

Men of the Day

THE SUCCESS of a city, not less than of a business corporation, is due to the intelligence, enterprise and energy of those who are at the head of its affairs, or who are identified with large interests within its confines.

The portraits and biographical outlines which appear upon the following pages are those of men who have, in a large measure, made Atlantic City and placed it foremost among the great resorts of America, if not of the world.

It is proper and appropriate that the names of such useful and influential citizens should be preserved in a work of this character which is intended as a permanent record of Atlantic City from the date of its inception to the present time, and which will be treasured in thousands of homes when this generation has passed away and the affairs of a still greater Atlantic City are entrusted to other men of, let us believe, equal sagacity and breadth.

Chalkley S. Leeds

THE subject of this sketch is well worthy of a leadership in the biography of the City by the Sea, as the representative pioneer of her domain. Born in 1824 at a place then called Absecon Beach, now known as Atlantic City, Chalkley S. Leeds is entirely a product and example of the oldest and best class of citizens. Descended from an old and prominent family—son of Jeremiah and Millicent Leeds—his early education was completed at his boyhood home, and the associations formed have proven of sufficient strength to keep him one of the steadfast citizens and prominent factors of Atlantic City's best progress. In 1854 Mr. Leeds was appointed the first Mayor of the then infant City, and at that time the entire voting population numbered about twenty-five. The primitive form of ballot receptacle, a cigar box, is one of the curious recollections of that period; and another original condition, not a sufficient number of citizens available to occupy the offices required by the City's charter, would doubtless cause some wonder in the minds of the present age when the average office has candidates beyond the possibilities of successful attainment. Filling many positions of trust, Mr. Leeds has been for twenty-five consecutive years City Treasurer, and further identified with many enterprises leading to the advancement of Atlantic City in the best and most conservative sense. His is the example of a busy and well-spent life, surrounded now by the best evidences of success and mellowing into the ripe old age of a citizen who holds the highest affection and esteem of his friends and neighbors, and in every sense deserves the reputation which comes by reason of its just desert, as a thoroughly honorable and representative citizen.

CHALKLEY S. LEEDS

Daniel Morris

BORN in Ireland in 1820, son of James and Rebecca Morris. Daniel Morris received his early education at Port Irlington, Queens County, Ireland, and was graduated from Carlow College, assuming his chosen vocation as a civil engineer. A belief in the future of America induced the young soldier of fortune to seek success in the promise of a new country, and to this type of pioneer our nation owes a constantly increasing debt of gratitude. Loyal to his adopted country and with a determination to achieve success, the early manhood of young Morris was marked with a series of struggles, a condition from which he finally carved success, and in every sense deserved it.

It is related as an incident in his early career in this country that he applied to the Pennsylvania Railroad Company's engineering department for employment in one of their most difficult departments—canal construction—where only the highest skill and personal reputation were the stepping-stones to preferment, and this candidate, a stranger and without reference, offered his services with this statement, that he could only refer to his work, as he was without acquaintances, but the young engineer had offered to the keen judges assembled in that office, a challenge which they immediately accepted.

In 1853, Daniel Morris located in Atlantic City, at a time when the present metropolis was but a small settlement amid the barren Jersey pines, with a turbulent ocean lapping the edges of a wonderful beach. A keen judgment as to future possibilities immediately convinced the young engineer that this apparent desert could be developed and he determined to locate there, with a firm belief that time would prove the wisdom of his choice, and during the following years he found most active employment in surveying the proposed town and gave the early corporation the inspiration for the famous and beautiful thoroughfares of to-day.

As a philanthropist, Daniel Morris has given substantial evidence of his spirit of benevolence, contributing to many Catholic institutions in recognition of the Mother Church, of which he was a consistent member, and probably the most enduring monument to his memory is found in the Orphan Asylum now approaching completion at Hopeville, New Jersey.

The "Morris Guards," a military organization of local fame, was founded by him and bears his name in evidence of the esteem of the members. As a holder of much Atlantic City real estate, the city proper has had the benefit of his financial enterprise and good business judgment, and every emergency has brought forward the ability of the keen man of affairs, which in our progressive age is always an element of conservatism and safety.

Atlantic City has many citizens of merit and prominence, but the subject of this short sketch, her representative, Daniel Morris, did her credit from the many-sided completeness of the essentially self-made man who, in the ripening years of his busy life, found time and opportunity to deserve the affection of his town by many acts of quiet, self-respecting benevolence and philanthropy.

Col. Daniel Morris died on the afternoon of December 21st, 1898, and a life was ended of one who never held an ignoble passion, of one who never wronged a human being. In his life the ideal business man was typified. His hand was as open as his heart. He lived a long life, in which good deeds were sown with unstinted hand and far reaching arm.

DANIEL MORRIS

Elias Wright

THE subject of this sketch was born June 22, 1830, in Durham, Greene County, New York, and is the son of Anson P. and Abigail Pierce Wright. His early education was begun at a country district school and was largely supplemented by hard study at home, coupled with considerable exercise as a student at farming on his father's farm. As a young man, General Wright began his struggle for prominence as a teacher of a country school, to which occupation he gave three years' faithful service. He located at Atlantic City, New Jersey, in March, 1852. His first vocation was that of a school teacher for several years, later taking up the science of civil engineering and surveying. At the outbreak of the war in 1861, he was instrumental in raising and equipping a company called the "Home Guards," of which he was commissioned Captain. Promptly after the Bull Run fight he took his company to Trenton, where they were mustered into the 4th New Jersey Regiment of Infantry, and General Wright accepted a position as 2d Lieutenant (the lowest commission in the army). After much re-organization, drilling and other military preparation, much of the duties of the soldier was gathered by these patriotic spirited men. Among the many other duties the General filled the office of Judge Advocate of several special Courts-Martial during these stirring times, and practically working his way up from the lowest ranks as a non-commissioned officer to a position of prominence and importance in military circles. Probably no man among the veterans remaining in the State of New Jersey has seen a more varied or peculiar career as an intrepid soldier and a warm advocate of President Lincoln's policy. Many incidents are related which vividly portray a strong decision of character and individuality which make successful men no matter what their vocation may be. Elias Wright's service during the rebellion is a record of which he may be justly proud, and the many attestations from his superior officers prove the opinion in which they held his courage and ability. General Wright entered the service as 2d Lieutenant of Company G, 4th New Jersey Volunteer Infantry, August 17, 1861. Promoted to 1st Lieutenant Company D, January 3, 1862. Captured at Gaines Mill, Virginia, June 27, 1862, and imprisoned in Richmond, Virginia. Exchanged August 5,

ELIAS WRIGHT

1862. Wounded at Crampton Pass, Maryland, September 14, 1862. Promoted to a Captaincy, December 1862; Major, June 1863; Lieutenant-Colonel, April 1864; Colonel, August 1864; Brevet Brigadier-General U. S. Volunteers, January 1865, and confirmed by the Senate at that time for gallant and meritorious services during the war. The following enumeration of army service will doubtless be of interest:

He was on duty near Washington, D. C. until March 7, 1862; moved to the Peninsula, April 4th; in action at West Point, Virginia, May 7th; Seven Days' battle, June 25th-July 1st; battle of Gaines Mill, June 27th, where he was captured and imprisoned at Libby Prison for seven weeks. He was in action again on the Plains of Manassas and Bull Run Bridge, August 27, 1862; battle of Chantilly, September 1st; Maryland Campaign, September 7th-20th; battle of Crampton's Pass, Maryland, September 14th, where in leading the advance in the charge up the mountain he was badly wounded. Battle of Antietam, September 16th-17th; battle of Fredericksburg, Virginia, December 13th-15th; Chancellorsville Campaign, April 28th-May 6th; battle of Salem Heights, May 3d-4th; expedition to South Mills, December 5th-20th, 1863; battle with Fitzhugh Lee's Cavalry, May 21st; battle of Challin's Farm, September 29th-30th; expedition against Fort Fisher in December, 1864, and January, 1865; at the surrender of Johnson's army near Durham, North Carolina, April, 1865; Provost-Marshall of New Berne, North Carolina, May and June 1865.

The brigade having been ordered to Texas he resigned and went home, and was immediately taken into service by his former employer, Stephen Colwell. General Wright held eight commissions in the volunteer army, two of them as Captain, and rising, as above stated, to the rank of Brevet Brigadier General of the U. S. Volunteers. Of these he asked only for the rank of Captain.

After the war was over he was assigned by Mr. Colwell as surveyor and engineer and partially as manager of Mr. Colwell's business, with headquarters at Weymouth, Atlantic County, New Jersey. He continued that work until 1873, when he was engaged by Joseph Wharton, of Philadelphia, to manage his estate of more than 100,000 acres of land in New Jersey, in which work he is still interested. His researches of the titles extend back to 1720, covering many owners and many conditions, with the result that great credit is due to the ability of General Wright. No other land owner in that

x

region has ever undertaken such a tremendous task, in the successful outcome of which the General takes a just pride. It is an enduring monument to his industry and energy and also to the tenacity of purpose of Joseph Wharton, who has saved much trouble for his successors by clearing up the titles and boundary lines in Southern New Jersey.

In politics the General is an uncompromising Republican, though he is opposed to voting in the field and still does not believe that soldiers, either volunteer or regulars, should be allowed so to vote.

General Wright is a believer in thorough education, but has no superstitious reverence for mere literary culture as contrasted with practical training in affairs. He believes in the employment of men and women equally as teachers, and yet is decided in his belief that our public school system suffers, not only from incompetent officers, but from an undue proportion of women teachers. He has never had the time nor the disposition to contend for political preferment, and has, therefore, held but few offices, but he has had sundry occasions to look into the accounts and doings of political henchmen, and he regrets the knowledge so acquired. He has no denominational affiliations.

Hon. Allen B. Endicott

ALLEN B. ENDICOTT was born in May's Landing, New Jersey, March 7th, 1857, and is the son Thomas D. and Ann Endicott. On his father's side he is a lineal descendant of Governor John Endicott, of Massachusetts, while on his mother's side the famous Pennington family of New Jersey is represented. He graduated from Peddie Institute in 1876, and in June, 1879, from the Law Department of the University of Pennsylvania, receiving the degree of LL. B. After having spent three years in the law office of Peter L. Voorhees, Esq., was admitted to the New Jersey bar in 1880. In June, 1881, he was married to Ada H., daughter of Rev. J. B. Davis, D.D., of Hightstown, New Jersey.

Mr. Endicott was elected Collector of Atlantic County in May, 1883, and held that office continuously until the spring of 1898, when he resigned. Has also held the office of City Solicitor since 1887, without regard to the political complexion of the City Council, and during that period he has successfully prosecuted many cases of great interest to Atlantic City. The most important, perhaps, were the condemnation for the city of the Consumers Water Company and the Atlantic City Water Works Company, and the contest in the Supreme Court and the Court of Errors and Appeals between Atlantic City on the one side and the Camden & Atlantic Railroad Company and the State of New Jersey on the other. This litigation lasted several years and resulted in a victory for the city, whereby the Camden & Atlantic City Railroad Company was compelled to pay to the city the assessment on $400,000 upon the trolley road on Atlantic Avenue instead of paying it to the State, as the Company had preferred to do. Judge Endicott has a large civil practice. Declining all criminal business, and only appearing in the Criminal Court twice of recent years, and on these occasions under the appointment of the Court to defend Robert Elder and John Rech, both indicted for murder. His saving the life of Robert Rech is conceded to be the greatest triumph achieved in the Criminal Court of Atlantic County.

Judge Endicott was prominent in the organization of the Union National Bank, and has been President of that Institution since its organization. On the 18th of January he was appointed by Governor Griggs, Law Judge of Atlantic County for the term of five years.

HON. ALLEN B. ENDICOTT

Hon. Charles Evans

CHARLES EVANS, son of Joel and Hannah Evans, Orthodox Friends, was born in Delaware County, Pennsylvania, in the year 1838, educated at Westtown Friends Boarding School, and took up farming for a livelihood. In 1867 he gave up farming and moved to Atlantic City, purchased the Seaside House, which, under his skillful management, together with many improvements, has made this house a favorite resort during both the summer and winter season.

Mr. Evans is connected with many prominent institutions of Atlantic City, having in 1881 organized the Atlantic City National Bank, of which he is President. This bank ranks as the first in New Jersey, and twenty-fourth in the United States.

Mr. Evans is Vice-President of the Country Club of Atlantic City, Hall Commissioner, one of the Governors of the Atlantic City Hospital, a Director in the Gas and Water Company, Vice-President of the Guarantee Savings Loan and Investment Company of Washington, D. C., and a member of the Union League Club of Philadelphia.

Mr. Evans has always contributed to the interests of Atlantic City, and has distinguished himself as an active and efficient promoter and protector of the interests entrusted to him.

HON⁰ CHARLES EVANS

George F. Currie
President Second National Bank.
President Atlantic Safe Deposit and Trust Company.

GEORGE F. CURRIE

Levi C. Albertson

LEVI C. ALBERTSON, was born in Smith's Landing, Atlantic County, New Jersey, December 6th, 1844, and is the son of Jonathan and Asenath Albertson. Was educated at the public schools of his native town and at Pennington Seminary.

Mr. Albertson has an enviable record of service in the Civil War. He enlisted in the U. S. Navy in 1864 and served on the U. S. S. "Kansas," North Atlantic Squadron, under Admiral D. D. Porter until the close of the war. He participated in the attacks on Fort Fisher in December, 1864 and January, 1865; at Dutch Gap on the James River, March and April, 1865; served with land forces at City Point in April of the same year, acted as guard of prisoners at the capture of Petersburg and vicinity, and was discharged at Philadelphia, June 12th, 1865.

Mr. Albertson has been actively identified in the Insurance and Real Estate business for eleven years; was postmaster of Atlantic City for eighteen years, and is at the present time Vice-President of the Second National Bank. He is actively interested in social and educational organizations, having filled the offices of school trustee and superintendent of public schools of Atlantic City. Is also a trustee of the Dock and Land Improvement Company, having lots located near the Inlet, and has also other large real estate connections. Mr. Albertson is a member and trustee of the Central M. E. Church, and is an ardent and loyal Republican in politics, and is one of Atlantic City's most popular citizens.

LEVI C. ALBERTSON

Lorenzo A. Down

WAS born in Downsville, Gloucester County, New Jersey, October 9th, 1839, is the son of Jessie and Catharine Kandel Down, was educated in the schools of his native town, and in December, 1886, located in Atlantic City, having previously resided for eleven years at May's Landing.

Mr. Down has held, for over thirty years, positions of honor and trust, was for eleven years Secretary and Treasurer, also a Director, of the Atlantic Safe Deposit and Trust Company, and at the present time is Cashier of the Second National Bank of Atlantic City, is also identified with numerous building associations located on the Jersey Coast, the owner of a handsome residence in Atlantic City, a block of stores in Vineland, New Jersey, and considerable real estate in other parts of Atlantic County, including dwellings at May's Landing and Holly Beach, and several cranberry bogs and farm lands.

Mr. Down has received numerous political honors, and for the past twenty years has filled various appointments and positions. He served as Township Clerk of Buena Vista Township, and Tax Collector thereof from 1869 until 1874, Clerk of Atlantic County 1875 to 1885, being the first County Clerk to secure the re-election, and from 1885 to 1890 was Deputy County Clerk. When elected Clerk of Atlantic County he received all the votes in the township in which he resided, excepting three.

Mr. Down is a consistent member of the Methodist Episcopal Church, and is at present a Trustee of the Central M. E. Church of Atlantic City.

In politics he has been a staunch and life-long member of the Republican Party.

LORENZO A. DOWN

Hon. Lewis Evans

LEWIS EVANS born in Estellville, Atlantic County, New Jersey, August 12th, 1842. Left home when fifteen years of age and settled first at May's Landing. Remaining there but a short time he then went to Camden, and engaged his services as messenger boy, carrying messages between that city and Philadelphia before the cable across the Delaware had been laid. In leisure moments he learned telegraphy and for three summers was sent out during the season as operator.

Gaining confidence in the young man from his faithfulness in these smaller matters the West Jersey & Seashore R. R. gave him the appointment of station agent at Atco. From there he was removed to a larger office in Hammonton, and later in 1863 came to this city, still in the position of agent. He remained in the railroad's employ until 1885, when he was elected County Clerk on the Republican ticket, this compelling him to resign the position of agent, holding the Clerkship until 1895.

His early interest in political affairs, perhaps, brought about the happy coincidence which led to his marriage to Miss Clara Leeds, daughter of Chalkley S. Leeds, the first man to hold position of Mayor of Atlantic City. Mr. Evans has a family of three daughters and one son.

Mr. Evans has held during his life in this city many offices of prominence and trust, being City Clerk for two years, many years in the Board of Education, and at the organization of the first Building and Loan Association to be formed in this place, was elected a Director, which position he still holds, together with position as Director of the Second National Bank.

Mr. Evans was one of the originators and incorporators of the Neptune Hose Company when organized in this city fifteen years ago, and has been its President successively since that time.

He is also a Past Master of Trinity Lodge, No. 79, F. & A. M., a Past Grand of American Star Lodge, I. O. O. F., and one of the originators of the Atlantic City Hospital, one of its Board of Governors, and its Treasurer.

Mr. Evans was elected State Senator at the last election. He has succeeded in making a happy combination of business success and social prominence which falls to the lot of but few men.

HON. LEWIS EVANS

XXIII

Hon. Joseph Thompson

JOSEPH THOMPSON was born at May's Landing, New Jersey, September 21st, 1853. Is the son of William W. and Hester T. Pennington Thompson. He was educated in his native town, studied law, and in the year 1878 was admitted to the New Jersey Bar.

In 1880, Judge Thompson located in Atlantic City, and since that date has been prominently interested in the financial and political progress of the City and County.

In May, 1881, Judge Thompson was elected Collector of Atlantic County, which office he held until May, 1883. In the year 1882 he was elected Solicitor for the Board of Chosen Freeholders of the County of Atlantic, being re-elected each year since that date. From April, 1882, to April, 1892, he ably served Atlantic County as Prosecutor of the Pleas, at the expiration of which term he was appointed Law Judge of Atlantic County, which position he held until April, 1898.

Judge Thompson's sterling integrity and marked personality have won him many friends and admirers, and although representing the minority party, he was in March, 1898, after an exciting contest, elected Mayor of Atlantic City.

Judge Thompson was one of the organizers of the Second National Bank of Atlantic City, also the Atlantic Safe Deposit and Trust Co., and has been a director and solicitor of both since their incorporation. He is also closely identified with other corporations of Atlantic City.

In March, 1898, he was appointed one of the managers of the State Hospital for Insane, at Trenton, and in July of the same year was appointed a member of the State Board of Taxation.

HON. JOSEPH THOMPSON

Alfred M. Heston

ALFRED M. HESTON, born at Hestonville, Philadelphia, April 30th, 1854, is the son of I. Morris and Anna Patton Heston. He was educated in Philadelphia, attending both the common and high school. He is descended from a family which located in Bucks County (Pennsylvania) during the time of William Penn, thus representing the sturdiness and strength of Quaker people, coupled with the native shrewdness which has made Bucks County famous.

Mr. Heston located in Atlantic City in 1884, and has contributed largely to the success of the city in whose progress he has shown great interest. He is an active and busy man; who for fifteen years edited and published a prominent daily paper; is fond of antiquarian and historical studies; author of various historical papers; author and publisher of Heston's Hand-Book of Atlantic City, and is at all times found at the head of any progressive movement which is to the advantage of his city. Active political connections have resulted in his filling the following offices: was a clerk in the House of Representatives during the 51st Congress; elected Comptroller of Atlantic City in 1895 (which office he still holds); appointed Commissioner of Sinking Fund by the Supreme Court of New Jersey in 1896, and coupled with many other connections in which his individuality has brought success and distinction. The Republican Party has reason to take credit in this representative of her best tenets. His earnestness and painstaking coupled with ability and tenacity of purpose, place his powers of accomplishment beyond the ordinary.

Mr. Heston is a Presbyterian, and is actively interested in the Atlantic City Hospital, whose beginning was entirely due to his efforts. His record as a public man is without blemish or reproach, and his ability as a scholar, student and writer extends far beyond the boundary of his city and state. Atlantic City is fortunate in having so worthy a son, and an earnest scholar to protect her best interests.

ALFRED M. HESTON

XXVII

Carlton Godfrey, Esq.

CARLTON GODFREY, son of Samuel and Martha (Carson) Godfrey, was born in Cape May County, N. J., January 13th, 1865, and received a public school education.

Mr. Godfrey read law with James B. Nixon of Atlantic City, and was admitted to the bar in November, 1889, and has since successfully practiced his profession in Atlantic City. In 1894 he formed a partnership with Burrows C. Godfrey under the firm name of Godfrey & Godfrey.

Mr. Godfrey is a Republican in politics, held the office of Tax Collector since 1893, for five successive terms, and each successive election has received an increased majority.

In March, 1898, was elected City Solicitor of Atlantic City, which position he still holds; his firm has represented the borough of Longport since its incorporation. He is, in addition to his active practice, closely identified with the corporation and other business interests of Atlantic City.

Mr. Godfrey is President of the Real Estate and Investment Company of Atlantic City, and has been Secretary of the Mutual Benefit and Loan Association for ten years, is also a member of the Board of Education.

CARLTON GODFREY, ESQ.

Burrows C. Godfrey

WAS born in Cape May County, N. J., July 22d, 1857, is the son of Leariney and Comfort L. Godfrey; received his early education in the schools of Cape May, and graduated from the American University, Tenn., with the degree of LL. B.

Mr. Godfrey taught school in Cape May and Cumberland counties, locating in Atlantic City in 1890, read law with Carlton Godfrey, Esq., and in 1894 was admitted to the bar. He was admitted as a Counsellor June term, 1897. In 1894 entered into partnership with Carlton Godfrey, forming the firm of Godfrey & Godfrey. He has successfully practiced his profession in Atlantic City since 1894, always social and pleasant, being a great favorite with those who know him.

BURROWS C. GODFREY

XXXI

James D. Southwick

JAMES D. SOUTHWICK, son of Joseph and Anna L. Southwick, was born December 25th, 1859, at Vincentown, New Jersey, and was educated in the public schools of his State.

By his generous and judicious management Mr. Southwick has made "The Shelbourne" (of which he has been proprietor for eighteen years) one of the foremost hotels of the island city, embodying all the comforts and entertainment which are appreciated by its many patrons.

Mr. Southwick is prominent in the management of the Atlantic City Hospital, which institution he has served in the capacity of Governor, has also acted as Secretary of the Country Club of Atlantic County, President of City Council, Chairman of the County Board of Elections, and is a Director of the Union National Bank.

In politics he is of Republication affiliations, and has received honor and office at the hands of his constituents. He is prominently known in religious circles as a communicant of the Episcopal Church

JAMES D. SOUTHWICK

XXXIII

Samuel Hastings Kelley

AS born in Philadelphia, Pennsylvania, and is the son of Elwood and Annie Kelley. His early education was obtained in the public schools of his native city. Mr. Kelley located in Atlantic City in the Spring of 1890, and became at once active in the development of this progressive city. The portion of this city known as Chelsea owes much of its development to his untiring energy; the improvements of the streets are also due to his unceasing advocation in that direction, appreciation of which is shown by many people who have erected beautiful cottages along these improved thoroughfares. Mr. Kelley was elected to City Council in 1897 for a term of three years.

Mr. Kelley is connected with the Protestant Episcopal Church, and is a staunch Republican in politics, but one of whom his opponents favor with the criticism " a shrewd and able friend, but a dangerous foe."

SAMUEL HASTINGS KELLEY

XXXV

Michael A. Devine

MICHAEL A. DEVINE was born in the city of Philadelphia, Pennsylvania, and moved early in life to Atlantic City, his father conducting at that time one of the first dry goods stores to be established on the Island, afterwards engaging in the hotel business. Mr. Devine was educated in the public schools and has always resided in Atlantic City. His first position in business was with the West Jersey Railroad Company, remaining with them about eight years, first in charge of the Express Department, and at the consolidation of the West Jersey and Camden & Atlantic Railroads held the position of Chief Clerk.

In 1891, Mr. Devine was elected to the office of Tax Collector and re-elected in 1892. In 1894, he organized the real estate, insurance and law firm of Devine & Wooton, whose prominence and ability has won for them many clients among the business houses of Atlantic City.

In July, 1896, Mr. Devine was appointed Postmaster of Atlantic City by President Cleveland, the Senate confirming the appointment in 1897.

Mr. Devine is largely interested in the development of real estate in the city, and actively identified with the Democratic Party in politics. He is a true representative of a progressive citizen, having many warm friends and admirers.

MICHAEL A. DEVINE

Judge Robert H. Ingersoll

IS the son of the late Doctor D. B. Ingersoll, a prominent county physician, and was born at May's Landing, New Jersey, November 17th, 1868. He graduated from the county public schools, and later attended Rutgers College. In 1884 he was appointed Page of the Senate, and in 1885, Assistant Journal Clerk, which position he filled until the close of the session in 1890, at which session he was the oldest officer in continuous service and the youngest in age.

Judge Ingersoll studied law with J. E. P. Abbott, Esq., of May's Landing, and Judge Endicott of this city. In 1890 he was admitted to the bar, and located in the Law Building—later, however, moved to his present office at South Carolina and Atlantic avenues.

He was Coroner of Atlantic County from 1892 to 1895, Alderman and President of City Council in 1895 and 1896, Recorder 1896 to 1898, and on February 28th, 1898, was appointed Judge of the District Court of Atlantic City for the term of five years.

Judge Ingersoll is an attorney of ability and prominence, has been identified with many progressive movements of Atlantic City, and his honest efforts have won for him the confidence of his constituents.

JUDGE ROBERT H. INGERSOLL

xxxix

Lewis Pennington Scott

LEWIS PENNINGTON SCOTT was born in Burlington, New Jersey, February 9th, 1854, is the son of John Hancock and Mary Pennington Scott. He received his early education at the public schools of Philadelphia.

Mr. Scott located in Atlantic City early in 1888, has been actively identified with the Republican Party and is at present time County Clerk of Atlantic County, having been elected in 1895 for a term of five years. He has a large and varied interest in real estate and is interested in the development of his adopted city.

Mr. Scott is a conservative, careful business man of sound principle and marked executive ability.

LEWIS PENNINGTON SCOTT

William H. Johnson

BORN in Port Republic, New Jersey, March 14th, 1853, and is the son of John W. and Sara Johnson, a prominent family of Atlantic County, largely interested in the cultivation of fertile farm land which has made the eastern portion of Atlantic County famous.

Mr. Johnson gained his early education at the place of his birth, Port Republic, and graduated from the County High School. He located in Atlantic City in 1875. In 1880 the Knickerbocker Ice Company absorbed the Norris and Peckert Company, of which Mr. Johnson was Manager, and subsequently installed him in that capacity in the new corporation. As a representative business man Mr. Johnson stands very high in the estimation of his business associates, representing one of the largest and most important branches of the famous Knickerbocker Ice Company. The success which has attended his management speaks highly of his ability to hold his Company's business in face of all competition.

Mr. Johnson owns considerable real estate in Atlantic City, and while not actively interested in politics, has always been a staunch adherent of the Republican Party.

WILLIAM N. JOHNSON

XLIII

Col. Geo. H. Perkins

GEORGE H. PERKINS was born in Boston, Massachusetts, July 12, 1846, and is the son of Geo. W. and Eliza S. Perkins; attended private schools until thirteen years of age, was then admitted to the Parks Street Grammar School, and later entered the High School in Portland, Maine, and in November, 1862, he enlisted in the army, and was assigned to Company H, 8th Maine Volunteer Infantry, then stationed at Beaufort, S. C. From this time until his discharge in November, 1865, Col. Perkins saw much actual campaigning, was present on a transport during the first bombardment of Ft. Sumter, from then on taking part in many hard fought engagements, and finally present at the surrender of General Lee at Appomattox Court House.

At the close of the war he took up his residence with his parents in Hammonton, N. J., and in 1874 came to Atlantic City, following the trade of carpenter for about ten years, after which he held various positions both in public and private enterprises, until his election in 1892 to the office of Justice of the Peace, which by a succession of re-elections he has since held. He has also been an active member in many of the secret societies of Atlantic City.

Since the foregoing memoir was written, and awaiting publication, Mr. Perkins died somewhat suddenly on Jan. 3d, 1899, at 2.30 A. M., aged fifty-two years. The news of his death was received with profound sorrow by his large circle of friends. His remains were laid at rest in the Pleasantville Cemetery on January 5th, 1899, with the funeral ceremonies of five secret orders to which he belonged.

COL. GEORGE H. PERKINS

XLV

John L. Young

JOHN LAKE YOUNG was born on the 25th of September, 1853, at Absecon, N. J., and is the son of James and Mary Ann Young. Has resided in this city since 1870, received his early education at Absecon, N. J. Mr. Young is a very successful man, and has always had a firm and abiding faith in the future of this city. He is a worker in every sense of the word, and has done much for the entertainment of the visitors to Atlantic City, erecting the first iron pier which proved of such great success that three others have since been erected. He is owner of much real estate.

JOHN L. YOUNG

XLVII

Charles R. Myers

CHARLES R. MYERS was born in the State of New Jersey, March 20th, 1859, is the son of George and Christine Myers. Was educated in New Jersey, and located in Atlantic City in 1876.

Mr. Myers is owner and proprietor of the Hotel Rudolf, which under his skillful management has become one of the most popular hotels in Atlantic City.

Mr. Myers is one of a family noted for its progressiveness and interest in the improvements and welfare of Atlantic City.

CHARLES R. MYERS

William Edgar Darnall, A. B., M. D.

IS the son of Henry Thomas and Margaret Pogue Johnston Darnall. He was born in Pearisburg, Giles County, Virginia. Place of early education, Durham, North Carolina, later graduating at Washington and Lee University, and at the University of Virginia.

Prior to studying medicine, Doctor Darnall served as private Secretary for several years to Gen. Custis Lee, and in May, 1896, located in Atlantic City. Doctor Darnall is prominent among the younger physicians of Atlantic City, and has already achieved quite a reputation as the writer of several treatises in connection with his profession. The "Fortnightly Club," composed of many of the leading literary people of Atlantic City, has had for its president Dr. Darnall. He is also a member and reporter of the Atlantic County Medical Society and the Academy of Medicine of Atlantic City. He is physician to the St. Michael's Baby Hospital, Visiting Physician to the Atlantic City Hospital, and Fellow of the American Academy of Medicine, also member of the Medical Society of New Jersey.

Doctor Darnall is a descendant of a prominent family of Virginia. He has genuine literary taste as a scholar and writer.

WILLIAM EDGAR DARNALL, A. B., M. D.

Wm. Blair Stewart, M. D.

AS born in Middle Spring, Cumberland Co., Penna., March 6th, 1867, is the son of Dr. William Graham Stewart and Martha Coyle Blair Stewart. Received his early education in the Chambersburg Academy, Penna.

Dr. Stewart graduated and received the degrees of Ph. B. and A. M., from Dickinson College, Carlisle, Pa. ; M. D. and M. D. Summa cum laude, from the Medico-Chirurgical College of Philadelphia, Pa. He located in Atlantic City in 1890, where he has since resided. His abilities have secured for him a large practice ; he has also achieved note as the author of "A Synopsis of the Practice of Medicine." He is Assistant Professor of Pharmacology and the Physiologic Action of Drugs in the Medico-Chirurgical College, Philadelphia, member American Academy of Medicine, American Medical Association, Ex-President Atlantic County Medical Society, and President Atlantic City Academy of Medicine.

Dr. Stewart is a member and Treasurer of the First Presbyterian Church, this city.

WM. BLAIR STEWART, M. D.

James North, M. D., D. D. S.

IS the son of the late Dr. Jos. H. North and Eliza H. Underwood, daughter of Hon. Jos. H. Underwood, of Fayette, Me. He was born in West Waterville (now Oakland) Kennebeck Co., Maine, Sept. 2d, 1855. He came to New Jersey in 1859 with his father, one of the first settlers at Hammonton, who was instrumental in building up that thriving village. He was educated in the public schools of that town, at the State Normal School at West Chester, Pa., and the Bryant & Stratton Business College in Philadelphia. He graduated from the Jefferson Medical College, Philadelphia, in 1880, and practiced the profession of medicine in Hammonton for two years with marked success, giving up the same for the profession of Dentistry, taking the degree of Doctor of Dental Surgery from the Philadelphia Dental College in 1883. He located in Atlantic City in the spring of that year, and has built up a large and lucrative practice. The Doctor is a member of many of the fraternal and social societies of the city, his speeches being models of beauty and eloquence, and as an orator has few equals. He enjoys the title of Poet Laureate of Atlantic County, though his reputation as a master of verse is not limited by its boundaries. The Doctor was married in 1883 to Miss Cora E. Faunce, and has two daughters.

JAMES NORTH, M. D., D. D. S.

Dr. J. F. Crandall

JOSEPH F. CRANDALL was born at Honesdale, Pennsylvania, in 1872. Graduated from the Pennsylvania Dental College at Philadelphia, and located in Atlantic City in the spring of 1896.

Doctor Crandall has acquired much reputation as a dental specialist, and endeavors by means of the best and most advanced appliances to banish that dread of the dental chair experienced more or less by all. He has, by years of extensive travel and successful experience, developed a proficiency of treatment, which, in connection with his close observance of sanitary regulations, warrants the highest possible results in his profession.

DR. J. F. CRANDALL

Dr. William Francis Seeds

BORN in East Bradford, Chester County, Pennsylvania, November 8th, 1852, and was educated in the public schools of East Bradford and at Unionville Academy. Mr. Seeds' early life was spent with his parents until he reached the age of twenty, when he entered the dental office of Doctor Jonathan Hisey, of Columbiana, Ohio, where he became an expert in extracting teeth, a specialty which has gained Doctor Seeds an extensive reputation. Doctor Seeds has had wide experience in Ohio, Pennsylvania and New Jersey, and has achieved among the profession an enviable position as an adept with the forceps. At present he is associated with Doctor Joseph F. Crandall in the Union National Bank Building.

Doctor Seeds has also been connected with the management of hotels here for many years, especially of later years with the hotel "Cedarcroft." He is a charter member of the Beach Pirates' Chemical Engine Company; Secretary of the Fire Wardens' Association, and a member of the Firemen's Relief Association.

In a quiet and conservative way, Doctor Seeds has always been identified as an influential Republican.

DR. WILLIAM FRANCIS SEEDS

Walter E. Edge

WALTER E. EDGE was born in Philadelphia, Pennsylvania, November 20th, 1873, and is the son of William Edge, of Downingtown, Pennsylvania. He was educated at Pleasantville, Atlantic County, New Jersey, and graduated from the public schools of Atlantic County, second in a class of fifty-two, in 1887. Mr. Edge moved from Pleasantville to Atlantic City in 1888, and served for four years on the staff of the "Daily Review." He was publisher and proprietor of the "Daily Guest" when twenty-one years of age, the youngest editor of a daily newspaper in the State. Afterwards, in 1895, changing the name of his paper to the Atlantic City "Daily Press." Mr. Edge is also proprietor of The Dorland Advertising Agency, which handles much of the advertising for Atlantic City and her hotels.

Mr. Edge, by reason of his untiring energy and marked ability, achieved success and prominence in the walks of journalism at an early age. He is at present Journal Clerk of the New Jersey State Senate, and is a member of the Atlantic City Republican Executive Committee. Mr. Edge is also a member of the "Morris Guards," having served as its President in 1895-6. Is Secretary of the Country Club of Atlantic City and likewise of the Pen and Pencil Club. He is prominent in the Masonic fraternity, a member of the Order of Elks and connected with the Atlantic City Hospital Association.

When the war with Spain commenced Mr. Edge offered his services and was commissioned a Lieutenant in Co. F, 4th New Jersey Volunteer Infantry (the former Morris Guards)—relinquishing business to serve the nation and served until the close of the war when he resigned his commission and returned to business.

Mr. Edge is interested in the development of Atlantic City and is the owner of considerable real estate. He is prominently identified with the highest and best interests of the city. As a representative citizen of Atlantic City, Mr. Edge is of the type which promises much for the future of this flourishing seaside resort.

WALTER E. EDGE

William McLaughlan

THE son of John and Jane McLaughlan, was born in Philadelphia, March 14th, 1866. His father contributed during life to the "Ledger" and other papers in Philadelphia and New York, and published books on the Slavery question before the Civil war.

Wm. McLaughlan located in Atlantic City in 1888, and started a small paper, the "Shoppers' Guide." In 1889 it was changed to "Merchants' Gazette," and later to the "Sunday Gazette," the only Sunday paper in Atlantic City. It is an influential Republican paper.

In 1895 Mr. McLaughlan was elected Coroner, and held office until 1898. He held the inquest in the great meadow wreck of 1896, which was the most disastrous railroad wreck in America.

Politically he is a staunch Republican, and is actively interested in advancing the success of the Republican Party. He is a member of the Atlantic City Lodge of Elks, and Pequod Tribe of I. O. R. M.

Mr. McLaughlan is a very successful promoter and speculator. He built the beautiful place known as Gramercy Place, introducing the idea of flower beds through the centre of streets. He changed the waste section of sand hills into a garden spot. He has also erected several fine cottages, and in many ways has helped to beautify the city.

WILLIAM McLAUGHLAN

LXIII

Major Lewis T. Bryant

MAJOR LEWIS T. BRYANT was born in Atlantic City, July 26th, 1874, and belongs to one of its honored pioneer families. His father, the late Hon. John L. Bryant, was one of the early promoters of Atlantic City, and always interested in the advancement of the resort. He was at one time Mayor of the city, and at various times held many public offices of trust, and at the time of his decease represented Atlantic County in the House of Assembly.

Major Bryant entered the Pennsylvania Military College at Chester, and after completing a full course graduated with the degree of Civil Engineer in the year 1891, being the youngest graduate from that institution from the date of its organization. After leaving college he returned to Atlantic City and commenced the active control of his hotel, the Waverly, and under his progressive management it has been very successful and enjoys the patronage of a large and select list of patrons. The Waverly is one of the oldest and thoroughly established hotels of the resort, it having been previously conducted by Captain Bryant's father, and later by his mother.

During the intervals between seasons Major Bryant studied law in the office of Judge Allen B. Endicott, and was admitted to active practice at the New Jersey bar in February, 1898.

Major Bryant was Captain of the Morris Guards, Atlantic City's leading military and social organization, for four years, and has also been prominently identified with other social and philanthropic organizations.

At the outbreak of the Spanish-American war the Morris Guards volunteered their services on the first call, but were not accepted. When the second call for troops was made they again volunteered and were among the first companies mustered into the United States service from the State of New Jersey, Major Bryant then receiving his commission as Captain of Company F, Fourth New Jersey Volunteer Infantry, and received his commission as Major on March 6, 1899, while in the field.

MAJOR LEWIS T. BRYANT

Frank A. Smith

FRANK A. SMITH was born in Philadelphia, January 5th, 1841. His father was an old resident, who was the first foreman of "The Philadelphia Press" in 1863, and acquired quite a reputation in newspaper circles.

Frank A. Smith located at Atlantic City, 1870, and achieved prominence and success through his connection and management of the Inlet Hotel—which association has won him many friends and acquaintances. He is identified with many fraternal orders, is a prominent thirty-second degree Mason, and is a well-known business man, whose success has been won by conservative judgment and fair methods.

FRANK A. SMITH

LXVII

John G. Shreve
Publisher "Atlantic Review."

LXVIII

JOHN G. SHREVE

LXIX

John Gouldey

JOHN GOULDEY was born in Philadelphia, Pa., on March 11th, 1827. Of all the hard workers for the interest and welfare of Atlantic City, who have been prominent for their unselfish efforts in the city's behalf, none is more worthy of praise than Ex-Alderman John Gouldey. He came to Atlantic City, June, 1867, and was elected to Council in 1869. Previously the City Council only held meetings during the summer; he advocated all-year meetings and reform, and was elected on that ticket. This Council did the first important work, and on the measures then passed depended much of the future of the now flourishing city. In 1870 he was one of the instigators of the petition for a boardwalk, and pressed the ordinance through Council. The petition was fought on account of the city having no funds for such purpose, but Mr. Gouldey insisted upon borrowing the sum needed, and five thousand dollars was borrowed from Joseph Piersall, a cottager. Thus again another step was taken toward the city's future.

In 1875 he was again elected to Council, and in 1883 was elected Recorder and Justice of the Peace. Through him as Recorder the City Treasury received its first money. He has been Justice of the Peace ever since.

Mr. Gouldey was the father of, and started the first secret order on the Island, the American Star Lodge, I. O. O. F., and is now Past Grand.

Mr. Gouldey has always been a hard and persistent worker for what he conceived to be the interest of the people.

JOHN GOULDEY

Daniel L. Albertson

BORN at Smith's Landing, N. J., July 1st, 1851, and located at Atlantic City, 1892, where he became prominently identified with the local interests of this community. Mr. Albertson comes of a family noted in the Republican politics of Atlantic county for many years, and has personally been the people's choice for many important offices—serving in the City Election Board as Township Clerk for Egg Harbor and City Clerk of Pleasantville, and more lately has successfully filled the duties as Overseer of the Poor.

He is prominently connected with the Order of Red Men and other social organizations.

DANIEL L. ALBERTSON

Robert B. Leeds

ROBERT B. LEEDS was born at Atlantic City, May 2d, 1828, then known as Absecon Beach, and is the son of Jeremiah and Millicent Leeds. He thus represents one of the original pioneers. He is a brother of Chalkley S. Leeds, and has been identified with him in the early development of Atlantic City.

Mr. Leeds was the first Treasurer of Atlantic City, and has been Alderman, Recorder, Tax Collector, together with numerous other public appointments.

He is connected with the Masonic Order, and is a prominent man in other fraternal and social organizations.

ROBERT B. LEEDS

LXXV

Gilbert S. Stimson

GILBERT S. STIMSON was born in Philadelphia, September 18th, 1845, and is the son of Joseph S. and Caroline S. Stimson. He was educated at the public schools of his native city, and is a graduate of the Philadelphia High School.

Mr. Stimson located in Atlantic City in 1884, and has been actively interested in and identified with hotel management, and was clerk for the season of '76 at the Sea Side House, and was later connected with Garden Hotel, but has since removed to Philadelphia.

Mr. Stimson is a representative of the successful hotel men who have contributed largely to the comfort and pleasure of numerous sojourners at the City-by-the-Sea.

GILBERT S. STIMSON

William P. Jones

WILLIAM P. JONES was born in Philadelphia September 8th, 1842. He is the son of Isaac and Anna C. Jones. Received his education in the Friends' Boarding School, Westtown, Pa.

Mr. Jones is the manager of the Glaslyn Hotel, and has a host of friends. He has met with deserved success since coming to Atlantic City.

WILLIAM P. JONES

LXXIX

John E. Mehrer

JOHN E. MEHRER was born in New York City, March 12th, 1845. He was educated at the Philadelphia High School, and located in Atlantic City in 1860. He is a thoroughly representative, progressive, generous business man, and is identified with the social, fraternal and sporting interests of both Philadelphia and Atlantic City; an active, enterprising man who has taken advantage of shrewd foresight in the rapid growth and value the real estate of Atlantic City has made. John E. Mehrer deserves credit for his firm belief in the future of this portion of the Jersey coast. He has large holdings at the Inlet, and his Pavilion is one of the really enjoyable points of interest of which thousands of sight-seers and visitors to Atlantic City have so delightful a recollection. Mr. Mehrer is an enthusiastic yachtsman, and has established a reputation for his fast boat and namesake. One of the exciting events in the history of the summer City-by-the-Sea is the annual yacht race in which everybody takes such keen interest, and which so frequently results in victory for the Mehrer colors, representing the "John E. Mehrer," commanded by Captain S. P. Gale.

He is identified with the Masonic Fraternity as a 32d degree Mason, and is also connected with numerous other organizations, is prominent in every movement; is the owner of much valuable real estate, and has a reputation for progression in improvements of the best and most lasting nature.

JOHN E. MEHRER

LXXXI

Harry Wootton

THE son of Henry and Anne J. Eldridge Wootton, descendants of old and distinguished families of the State of Pennsylvania, was born in Atlantic City, October 30th, 1869; Mrs. Wootton being a daughter of Lemuel Eldridge, one of the founders of the late publishing firm of Henry B. Mann & Company, afterwards Barnes & Company, of New York City.

Mr. Wootton attended the public schools of Atlantic City, was graduated from the Atlantic City High School in the class of 1886, studied law under the tutorage of Honorable Joseph Thompson, was a member of the Class of '93 School of Law, Columbia College, and later in 1892 received the degree of LL. B. from the New York Law School.

Mr. Wootton has resided in Atlantic City since his birth, and as a successful attorney and progressive man of business has achieved prominence and distinction. Now on the side of life where work is not the main purpose, we find him again taking a prominent stand as in 1893-94 he served as Commodore of the Corinthian Yacht Club, and for many years an active member of the "Morris Guards." He is also connected with many secret societies, and is a member of the Atlantic City Country Club.

Coming as he has from staunch Republican stock, we find him actively interested in the success of his favorite party.

The Wootton family own a great amount of real estate in Atlantic City, and Mr. Wootton devotes much of his time to real estate matters, being a member of the firm of Devine & Wootton, who are prominently known throughout the State. He has practised law since June, 1892, and has been identified in the best sense with the progressive developments of his native city. He is a grandson of Jonah Wootton, Sr., owner of one of the pioneer hotels of Atlantic City, the Light House Cottage, which was afterwards moved to become part of the old Saint Charles Hotel, the site of which now forms part of St. Charles Place.

HARRY WOOTTON

S. A. Schweisfort

MR. SCHWEISFORT was born in Montgomery County, Pennsylvania, and located in Atlantic City in 1880.
As proprietor of the "Little Brighton," a hotel of note, restaurant and buffet he has achieved popularity and success. He is a thoroughly conservative business man, and with foresight and consideration for his patrons has made for his house an enviable reputation.

Mr. Schweisfort has been connected with the best developments of Atlantic City; is interested in all its improvements, and is a man of many friends.

S. A. SCHWEISFORT

LXXXIV

John Myers

JOHN MYERS, born in Philadelphia, May 10th, 1854, located at Atlantic City in 1876, and with his brothers established the famous Union Market. By attention to details and perseverance, success has been attained and the firm of Myers Brothers are types of business men who have demonstrated the value of fair dealing, good judgment and generous treatment of their patrons.

JOHN MYERS

Daniel W. Myers

THE subject of this sketch is a native of New Jersey, and a graduate of the High School of Atlantic City. He is an active business man and is identified with his brothers in the ownership of the Union Market. He is connected with the "Morris Guards," and is interested in the development and ownership of valuable real estate in Atlantic City, and is connected with numerous fraternal and social associations of the island.

Mr. Myers is a successful business man, and has been prominently identified with the improvements and progress of his city.

DANIEL W. MYERS

LXXXIX

Jacob C. Myers

A NATIVE of New Jersey, and received his education in the schools of Atlantic City. He is the son of George and Christine Myers, and connected with his brothers in the ownership of Union Market.

Mr. Myers has large real estate interests in Atlantic City and is a firm believer in the future developments of this locality. Is also prominently identified with the Masonic Order and other social organizations.

JACOB C. MYERS

Harry W. Sherrick

HARRY W. SHERRICK was born in Bellefonte, Pennsylvania, in 1875, graduated from Bellefonte Academy and Preparatory School for State College. He located in Atlantic City May 30th, 1893.

Mr. Sherrick is prominently connected with the Morris Guards and other fraternal and social organizations. He was formerly identified with the Atlantic City Railroad Company and is now cashier of the United States Express Company at Atlantic City. Mr. Sherrick is deservingly popular among the younger element of Atlantic City.

HARRY W. SHERRICK

XCIII

Devoux B. Edwards

DEVOUX B. EDWARDS was born in Bridgeton, New Jersey, May 13th, 1864, and received his early education from private tutors and in the South Jersey Institute. He located in Atlantic City in 1883, establishing the well-known "Floral Hall" and beautiful conservatories covering about eight thousand (8000) square feet, with all modern appliances for the propagation and growing of plants. Mr. Edwards deserves great credit by reason of the beautiful gardens which every summer, under his care, adorn the lawns in front of the "Brighton," "Traymore," "Haddon Hall," "St. Charles," and the fronts of many private residences and public squares.

Mr. Edwards is connected fraternally with the Masonic Order, Knights Templars, Odd Fellows, and is a member of the Morris Guards. He is a young man of ability and enterprise and as a business representative his methods are original and progressive.

DEVOUX P. EDWARDS

1. Wilden Moore

WILDEN MOORE was born in Bridgeton, New Jersey, in 1867, and is the son of George and Hatty T. Moore. He received his early education at Bridgeton and graduated from the high school at that place.

Mr. Moore located in Atlantic City in 1890. He came to Atlantic City rich in ambition, but poor in worldly goods, and has amassed a fortune by real estate investments and other legitimate enterprises. He is prominent as an importer in works of modern art, and his researches extend to Austria, France, Italy, etc., etc. He has a large patronage of the best and most critical class of our citizens coming from all parts of the country. Mr. Moore's establishment has excited favorable comment from thousands of visitors to Atlantic City.

Prominent among his fraternal connections we name the Order of Elks and the Odd Fellows. Mr. Moore has many friends, is a conservative, yet generous, citizen, and generally prominent in the affairs of Atlantic City.

J. WILDEN MOORE

XCVII

Roland Conrow

BORN in Cinnaminson, Burlington County, New Jersey, in 1871, and is the son of Clayton and Mary S. Conrow. He received his education at a private school and later at Swarthmore College, Pennsylvania. Mr. Conrow located in Atlantic City in 1896, and has established on Atlantic Avenue one of the most attractive as well as successful high grade grocery and provision markets to be found in the entire city. Mr. Conrow is a thoroughly progressive and able business man. To him also is due the credit of having built the first modern Apartment House in the City by the Sea—a handsome brick building at States and Atlantic Avenues. This design of building has since become very popular and is much appreciated as a departure from the old style of architecture.

ROLAND CONROW

XCIX

Edwin Smith

EDWIN SMITH was born in Philadelphia, November 21st, 1858, son of Edwin A. and Lavinia Russell Smith, and received his education from the public schools of his native city; entered active business life as a member of the firm Edwin A. Smith & Son, lime, cement, builders' supplies, an old Philadelphia house established in 1822. In 1884 Mr. Smith located in Atlantic City, and later became prominently identified with the Morris Guards, serving as Captain until 1891, when added business responsibilities compelled his retirement. Conservative in temperament, yet confident when conditions warrant progress, the subject of this sketch is a representative type of the men who have added much to the prosperity of Atlantic City.

EDWIN SMITH

Howard G. Harris, C. E.

HOWARD G. HARRIS, C. E., born in Tuckahoe, New Jersey, October 16th, 1871, son of Gilbert and S. Frances Harris. Received his early education through public schools of Atlantic County, gained a State Scholarship and paid his expenses through college by outside employment, took the engineering and scientific course and was graduated from Rutgers College, New Brunswick, New Jersey—and within the past few years associated himself with the firm of Harris & Company, combining real estate, civil engineering and a general business office. The success achieved by the new firm is attributed to fair methods and systematic business forms.

Mr. Harris believes in the future development and growth of Atlantic City.

HOWARD G. HARRIS, C. E.

Frank Middleton

FRANK MIDDLETON was born in New Britain Township, Bucks Co., Pa., January 25th, 1861, and is the son of Barclay and Emma E. Middleton. He received his education in the public schools of Montgomery County and Philadelphia, Pennsylvania. Mr. Middleton located in Atlantic City in 1881, but in 1882 moved to Albany County, N. J., and returned to Atlantic City in 1891 as assistant surveyor with Gen. Elias Wright, with whom he is still connected.

He is a member of the firm of H. G. Harris & Co., combining the real estate business with his profession as surveyor. Mr. Middleton ran the line for the county road from Hammonton to Absecon, and has completed a survey for the completion of the drive from Atlantic City to Longport.

FRANK MIDDLETON

Oliver H. Guttridge

OLIVER H. GUTTRIDGE was born in Nottingham, England, May 2d, 1842, attended the public schools of Nottingham and graduated from Queenstown College. Mr. Guttridge is a lineal descendant of General Smallwood, who was especially noted in the war of the French Revolution.

He located in Atlantic City in 1878, has many social connections, and as a charter member is actively identified with the Order of Elks. Mr. Guttridge conducts a successful business as a general contractor, owns valuable real estate in Atlantic City and is favorably known as an enterprising, progressive business man.

OLIVER H. GUTTRIDGE

Albert M. Jordan

ALBERT M. JORDAN was born in Auburn, New York, July 20th, 1847, and received his early education at Independence, Iowa, finally attending Cornell College, Mount Vernon, Iowa, but owing to the death of his father (then doing active service in the War of the Rebellion) he was prevented from graduating as a Mechanical and Civil Engineer.

Mr. Jordan upon leaving college became identified with the printing business in Philadelphia, but not being satisfied with the results, migrated west, and located in Dubuque, Iowa, becoming identified for several years as part owner in the "Dubuque Daily Times." Later, in 1883, Mr. Jordan came east and located in Atlantic City, and shortly afterwards secured from Council an Ordinance for a Sewerage Company, and helped to construct the plant. He was Superintendent from the time of its inception until 1897, when he was elected President and General Manager, which position he now fills.

Mr. Jordan is largely interested in the Robinson Land Company, has long been identified with the Republican Party and is a thoroughly representative business man of Atlantic City.

ALBERT M. JORDAN

CIX

C. G. Johnson

C. G. JOHNSON was born in Absecon, New Jersey, March 27, 1872, and is the son of C. P. and Silvia Johnson. He received his early education in the public schools of his native town and in Atlantic City, locating at the latter place about 1892.

Mr. Johnson is a successful wholesale manufacturer and dealer in white lead and painters' supplies, having a large factory at Pleasantville, N. J. He is also connected with fraternal and social organizations of the city, and is a member of the Reserve Hook and Ladder Company.

C. G. JOHNSON

Henry C. Eldridge

WAS born in Chester County, Pennsylvania, and is the son of Samuel Eldridge, one of the pioneer cottagers of Atlantic City, who was favorably known and highly honored as an old sojourner. Mr. Eldridge located in Atlantic City in 1857 and was educated in the public schools. He early became identified with the Police Department and secured an appointment as a Patrolman, finally working his way up to Chief-of-Police, which appointment he still retains.

Chief Eldridge is noted for courage and quiet manliness. He has probably made some of the most exciting history of the city, but disclaims all unnecessary publicity or credit and quietly goes on his path of duty.

Chief Eldridge is a staunch Republican in politics and in a modest way has acquired prominence in real estate and other interests.

WILLIAM M. POLLARD, PRESIDENT
CHARLES B BOYER, VICE-PRESIDENT

RAYMOND P. READ, SECRETARY
JOHN F. TURNER, TREASURER

THE MUTUAL BUILDING AND LOAN ASSOCIATION
100 GUARANTEE TRUST BUILDING
ATLANTIC CITY, N. J.

November 19, 1923.

Mr. A. H. Phillips,
Phila. Pa.

My dear Mr. Phillips:-

    This is to advise you that Chief Eldredge's father's name was Lemuel.

    Yours very truly,

HENRY C. ELDRIDGE

Benjamin Williamson

BENJAMIN WILLIAMSON was born in Glassboro, New Jersey, May 6th, 1858. He was educated in the public schools of Atlantic City and Philadelphia, and resided in Atlantic City for thirty-eight years. He was identified with the Fire Department for twenty years and was elected its Chief on January 18th, 1897. Mr. Williamson contracted pneumonia while attending to his duties, at the fire of the Currie Hardware Co., Christmas Eve, 1897, and died on January 10th, 1898, closing a busy and active life, but the memory of his many sterling qualities and attainments has endeared him to his friends. He gave the best years of his life to the development and success of the Fire Department of Atlantic City, and largely through his efforts the reputation of Atlantic City's Fire Department has reached fame and distinction.

BENJAMIN WILLIAMSON

Charles M. Speidel

CHARLES M. SPEIDEL was born in Schoeneich, Wurtemberg, Germany, March 5th, 1862, at the old homestead or family seat of the Speidel Muehle, who for generations have been noted millers. He is the son of J. G. and Kate Speidel, and received his early education in the public schools of Germany.

Mr. Speidel located in Atlantic City February 17th, 1890, and is proprietor and owner of Hotel "Speidel," located on Atlantic Avenue, and is identified with the Masonic organizations and is a member of the Atlantic City Fire Co., No. 2, of which company he has been elected for the third time as Trustee, and in 1894 as Foreman of the Company, and for his unremitting energies for past years, was elected by the entire Atlantic City Fire Department in 1897, as one of their superior officers.

CHARLES M. SPEIDEL

CXVII

John Donnelly

JOHN DONNELLY was born in Philadelphia May 14th, 1848, and is the son of Dominick and Catherine Donnelly. He was educated in Philadelphia, and is a graduate of the Philadelphia High School.

Mr. Donnelly located in Atlantic City in 1890, and is actively interested in the development of real estate and interests which mean the betterment of the city.

Mr. Donnelly is agent for the Philadelphia Brewing Company, and has been successful in every sense. He is a member of the Catholic Knights, Order of Red Men, Elks and City-by-the-Sea Society, has many friends, is conservative but loyal to the best interests of his adopted city.

JOHN DONNELLY

Samuel W. Moore

SAMUEL W. MOORE was born in Bridgeton, New Jersey, June 12th, 1870, and is the son of George W. and Hettie T. Moore. He attended school at Bridgeton, and graduated from the West Jersey Academy.

Mr. Moore located in Atlantic City in 1890, engaging in the real estate business, of which he made a great success. He later went into the hotel business, and is now proprietor of the Waldorf-Astoria, a new hotel just completed on the beach. This modern hotel is the result of his untiring energies, and is proof of his knowledge of the hotel business.

He is a member of the Sons of American Revolutionary Society, his great-grandfather having been an officer in the Revolutionary War.

Mr. Moore is largely interested in real estate personally, and is prominent in social circles, having an extensive acquaintance and many friends.

SAMUEL W. MOORE

Jacob Mueller

WAS born at Elsas, Germany, in 1861, attended the public schools of his native country for ten years, and came to this country in 1878. He resided in Montgomery Co., Pa., for six years; in Philadelphia, Pa., three years; moving to Atlantic City in 1887.

He is prominently connected with the Odd Fellows, Knights of the Golden Eagle, Red Men, Elks, Volunteer Fire Department, and is an honorary member of the Pen and Pencil Club; also, is an active member of the Turn Verein and the Mannerchor.

Mr. Mueller is a progressive hotel keeper of Atlantic City, and has achieved a reputation for the management of his house and careful consideration of his guests and patrons.

JACOB MUELLER

Oliver Merchant

THE subject of this sketch was born in Devonshire, England, in 1854, and was educated in a private school in his native town.

Mr. Merchant located in Atlantic City in 1894, and has established and successfully conducted the famous Merchant's Cafe and Restaurant, which has achieved quite a reputation in Atlantic City. He has had a wide and varied experience in the care of his patrons, and he was for many years steward on the famous vessels of the White Star Line plying between New York and Liverpool. He also successfully managed the "Iroquois House," a famous mountain resort on the Belveil mountains, St. Hiliare, Province of Quebec, Canada, and superintended the building and equipping of the St. George Club, Sherbrooke, Quebec, Canada, which institution he successfully managed for upwards of three years and left it one of the most successful institutions of its kind in Canada.

He is actively interested in many of the fraternal associations, prominent of which may be mentioned the Masonic Order, Elks, Odd Fellows, Ancient Order United Workmen, Sons of St. George and Red Men. He is also interested in the management of the Atlantic City Hospital.

Mr. Merchant feels a deep interest in the welfare of his adopted city.

OLIVER MERCHANT

Samuel P. Gale

SAMUEL P. GALE was born in Tuckerton, New Jersey, August 24th, 1855, and being the son of an old sailor, in early life developed for himself a fondness for "old ocean." He located in Atlantic City in 1859, where he received his early education.

Probably no man in Atlantic City is better known than Captain Gale—fisherman, sailor, man of affairs. He has friends innumerable. As skipper of the new champion yacht "John E. Mehrer Second," Captain Gale has won renown. The John E. Mehrer Second was designed and sailed by Mr. Gale and his brother, and won the championship in the match race against the St. Charles.

He is a charter member of the Order of Elks, and is actively known among the yachtsmen of the Jersey Coast.

SAMUEL F. GALE

CXXVII

Lewis R. Adams

LEWIS R. ADAMS was born in Atlantic City, January 10th, 1863, and is the son of Alfred and Clara Adams. He received his early education at the Penn Avenue School House, Atlantic City. He learned the trade of bricklayer and plasterer, and worked on most of the important buildings of this city.

Mr. Adams was the first Building Inspector elected by the Atlantic City Council, holding the office for some years. He made a good and very popular city official.

Mr. Adams has been in the bath business for nine years, is Republican and was for four successive years Chairman of the City Executive Committee.

LEWIS R. ADAMS

William G. Generotzky

WILLIAM G. GENEROTZKY was born in Bickfeld, Westphalia, Prussia, Germany, August 28th, 1852, and is the son of Henrich G. and Dorothea Generotzky. He was educated in the public schools of his native country, located in Atlantic City in 1881, and in 1891 established himself in the business of baker, in which Mr. Generotzky has had a prominent and successful career.

He is connected with most of the lodges in Atlantic City in a fraternal and social sense. Possessed of quiet determination and considerable business ability, he has, by hard work and perseverance, reached his present successful position.

WILLIAM G. GENEROTZKY

CXXXI

William F. Wahl

WILLIAM F. WAHL was born in Boston, Massachusetts, December 10th, 1853, attended the public schools of his native city and located in Atlantic City in 1872.

Mr. Wahl has been for over twenty-five years one of Atlantic City's most successful merchants, having probably the best representative store on the Jersey coast.

Mr. Wahl is the owner of much real estate and is actively interested in the development of Atlantic City. He has built and occupies a residence noted for its good taste and quiet beauty.

WILLIAM F. WAHL

CXXXIII

James Daley

BORN in Baltimore, Md., July 19, 1855, and located at Atlantic City in 1886. Mr. Daley became identified with the commercial interests of his town, and established himself prominently in the manufacture of cigars and smokers' articles, and his store is thoroughly representative of the best class. Active socially, but of conservative habit, and thoroughly interested in the welfare of his adopted city, he is, in every sense, a self-made man.

JAMES DALEY

Rev. J. J. Fedigan, O. S. A.

FAMOUS in the history of Atlantic City by reason of his fidelity to his parish, and the rare good humor and racy wit which marked his intercourse with the events of the past years. Higher honors have called him from his old field, but his memory will ever be endeared to the people of Atlantic City as a scholar and man of rare integrity.

REV. J. J. FEDIGAN, O. S. A.

CXXXVII

Edward S. Lee

IS a well-known business man of Atlantic City whose interests have aided the development of many improvements. Mr. Lee has been in close touch with the political growth of his city and has served in several official connections.

EDWARD S. LEE

CXXXIX

Hon. F. P. Stoy

EX-MAYOR of Atlantic City, and prominently connected with many social and political organizations of his community.

HON. F. P. STOY

George C. Felker

LOCATED at Atlantic City in 1885 and established a noted decorative and designing house in his adopted city. Mr. Felker is a careful and industrious business man and worthy of success.

GEORGE C. FELKER

Thomas K. Reed, M. D.

PHYSICIAN, author and scientist. One of the most prominent in the medical fraternity of Atlantic County.

THOMAS K. REED, M. D.

Thomas J. Dickinson

ONE of the prominent merchants of Atlantic Avenue, noted for fair dealing and liberal treatment. Interested in everything of real value in the promotion of Atlantic City's real progress, yet always safe through conservative judgment of the best and most prudent course.

THOMAS J. DICKINSON

Emery D. Irelan

PROMINENT officially in the affairs of Atlantic City, he has filled many important offices, and has a large circle of acquaintances. One of the representative younger men of his community.

EMERY D. IRELAN

CXLIX

I. G. Adams

NE of Atlantic City's prominent real estate operators who has been identified with the growth of his city.

J. G. ADAMS

S. B. Rose

THE subject of this sketch is prominently identified with the commercial interests of Atlantic City and has been successful in his field. Mr. Rose represents progress and a practical knowledge of affairs.

S. B. ROSE

CLIII

J. J. Rochford

ORMERLY of a famous sanitarium located in Atlantic City and more lately identified with numerous mechanical and industrial inventions.

CLIV

J. J. ROCHFORD

Thomas K. Wilson

THE subject of this sketch is a conservative business man of Atlantic City, and has been identified with many of the commercial interests of his locality, prominent of which is the distributing of the dairy products of Atlantic County. Mr. Wilson has a large circle of friends and is connected with several social affiliations.

THOMAS K. WILSON

Samuel Barton

 PROMINENT citizen of Atlantic City who has been connected with many improvements and permanent interests of his locality.

CLVIII

SAMUEL BARTON

George B. Long

THE subject of this sketch is a deservedly popular business man, and has established a valued and important personal connection with the local interests of Atlantic City.

GEORGE H. LONG

H. C. Baney

PROMINENT in local affairs and noted for his social and fraternal connections, the subject of this sketch is a progressive representative of Atlantic City.

H. C. BANEY

CLXIII

Theo. Gross

IS a popular business man of prominent social connections, noted for his genial disposition. Mr. Gross has been identified with the many improvements of Atlantic City and has a large circle of acquaintances.

THEO. GROSS

C. Garrabrant, M. D.

A PROMINENT and successful physician of Atlantic City, whose ability has placed him in the front ranks of his profession, and who has a strong interest in the welfare of his locality.

C. GARRABRANT, M. D.

S. C. Taylor

S. C. TAYLOR is a prominent gentleman, largely interested in the business prosperity of Atlantic City and the many architectural improvements connected with the phenomenal growth of his locality. Mr. Taylor is successful and affable, and has a large circle of acquaintances.

S. C. TAYLOR

CLXIX

Carl Voelker

AS born in Neiderbraun, Alsace, Germany, May 20th, 1855, and is the son of Christian and Magdalene Voelker. He received his education in Germany and later in Buffalo, N. Y., having moved with his parents to the latter place before the German-Franco war.

He moved to Egg Harbor City after the Philadelphia Centennial, and later, in 1882, formed a connection with "The Times" of Atlantic City as journalist, locating permanently in the latter place in 1882. Following his chosen profession he became editor of the "Atlantic City Frie Press," which, under his able management since 1891, has become an influential paper among the German-American element.

Mr. Voelker is a prominent and influential member of the Democratic Party; is a member of the Democratic County Executive Committee; ex-member of the Board of Education, on which board he served eight years, four of which as Secretary.

Mr. Voelker has been connected with Schauffler's Hotel more or less since 1880 as chief clerk, and in 1897, when the city purchased the property for a City Hall site, he was proprietor.

He was one of the organizers of the A. C. Maennerchor and the A. C. Turnverein, and generally recognized as a factor among the German-American element in city and county.

Mr. Carl Voelker is also local agent for the North German Lloyd Steamship Co.

J. C. Smith

IS noted for careful and conservative business judgment, and during the past years has had a large commercial interest in the wholesale produce trade of Atlantic City.

Herbert McCann

THE subject of this sketch was prominently identified with the famous Boardwalk interests of Atlantic City, and a pioneer in the ocean pier construction, which has added so much pleasure to thousands of visitors of the past years.

William A. Bell

WILLIAM A. BELL is a member of a progressive firm of enterprising merchants located on Atlantic avenue, who have been largely identified with the commercial interests of Atlantic City.

John L. Gorman

JOHN L. GORMAN is associated with his partner, William A. Bell, and their firm is deservedly popular, representing a large and constantly increasing business in their general department store.

Frank A. Souder

FRANK A. SOUDER is a successful builder and has large property interests in Atlantic City. He has risen to a prominent position in his profession, and has been interested in every large operation throughout this community.

M. Walton

PROMINENTLY connected with the commercial interests of Atlantic City, and has the gratification of achieving merited success as the representative of the famous Abbott Dairies, known throughout Atlantic County for their cream products. Mr. Walton is a self-made man, of genial temperament, and has a large social and business acquaintance throughout his community.

www.ingramcontent.com/pod-product-compliance
Lightning Source LLC
Chambersburg PA
CBHW031417230426
43668CB00007B/339